WHAT PEOPLE ARE SAYING:

The women of the Bible have been miscast for centuries as demons, harlots, and jezebels—and intentionally so. For if the truth about who these women were and what they represented were more widely known, it would challenge most of the assumptions we have about Judaism and Christianity. Dr. Trimble-Familetti has provided an invaluable service with this book, one that may have lasting legacy in Biblical scholarship.

—Reza Aslan, International Best Selling Author of *Zealot: The Life and Times of Jesus of Nazareth* and *No god but God*

That Dr. Trimble-Familetti's work covers such diverse ground makes the book a unique and worthwhile read, and those eager to investigate the real place of women in religion would be well directed toward this text.

—Foreword Reviews

This book is exactly what it claims to be—"a call for biblical literacy"—including details about women that are often overlooked or intentionally erased from religious discourse . . . Trimble-Familetti's respect for biblical evidence makes for outstanding reading.

—Virginia R. Mollenkott, Ph.D., Stylistic Consultant, *The New International Version of the Bible* and Author of *Women, Men and the Bible* and *The Divine Feminine*

Women have always played a vital role in religion and society. The Bible tells us so, as this book so artfully demonstrates. Those of us committed to communicating this will be grateful for this resource. Ideal for small group discussions.

—Miriam Therese Winter, Ph.D.,
Professor, Hartford Seminary

Although often silenced, forgotten or misrepresented, female characters of the Bible were crucial to the early development of Christianity. Dr. Trimble-Familetti researches and shares the true roles of women . . . for us to see the importance for our lives of these often maligned women.

—Rev. Dr. Shannon Clarkson,
Co-editor *The Dictionary of Feminist Theologies*,
and *Just Hospitality: God's Welcome in a World of Difference*

With skill and insight, Dr.Trimble-Familetti brings to life many overlooked and under-valued women in the Bible. Their voices invite new—and sometimes challenging—ideas to emerge. If you read only one book this year, I hope it will be this one!

—Dr. Kendra Weddle Irons,
2013–2014 Coordinator, Evangelical and
Ecumenical Women's Caucus-Christian Feminism Today

Dr.Trimble-Familetti fills in the missing pieces of (Biblical women's) lives and provides some thought-provoking tidbits that will pique your interest. A powerful educational resource for all who would like to know biblical women in a whole new way.

—Dr. Bridget Mary Meehan,
Association of Roman Catholic Women Priests, Author of
Living Gospel Equality Now and *Praying With Women of the Bible*

Trimble-Familetti's remarkable book is a gift to all, and one that courageously invites everyone to ask questions, as well as to adopt a more noble and just view of how men and women can live and work together today.

—Joyce A. Kovelman, Ph.D.,
Author of *Crimes Against Humanity: A1H1W2*

Dr. Trimble-Familetti did exhaustive research and sets the record straight regarding women (in the bible) . . . The outcome is stunning, and shoots down many of the misconceptions the casual Bible reader may have about these historical—and often powerful—women.

—John De Salvio,
Author of *God Told Me to Draw These*

An impressive contribution to our understanding of Scripture. Trimble-Familetti has hit upon a simple and yet powerful way to let the women of Scripture speak, plainly and boldly . . . with a particularly fine flair for expression and the priceless gift of empathy.

—Rev. Roger Schriner,
Author of *Bridging the God Gap*

Ah—at last—Balance! A refreshing and fascinating biblical exegesis from the woman's perspective. Insightful and revealing for both women and men! Dr. Trimble-Familetti's book enriches and balances our shared biblical story.

—Edwina Gateley, Poet, Author,
Public Speaker, Women's Advocate

PROSTITUTES, VIRGINS AND MOTHERS

Questioning Teachings About Biblical Women

DR. PAULA TRIMBLE-FAMILETTI

For information about this title or to order other books and/or electronic media, contact the publisher:

Personhood Press
PO Box 370, Fawnskin, CA 92333
www.personhoodpress.com
info@personhoodpress.com

Library of Congress Control Number: 2013913733
ISBN: 978-1-932181-95-1 Trade Paper (softcover)
ISBN: 978-1-932181-98-2 Kindle Ebook
ISBN: 978-1-932181-97-5 PDF
ISBN: 978-1-932181-96-8 EPub

Disclaimer:
The author and publisher are not engaged in rendering religious or spiritual advice and have no intent to offend any person or religion whose views may differ. Our intent is to offer alternative interpretations of the stories of selected biblical women. Read this book at your own risk if you are a strong believer that traditional interpretations of biblical women are the only absolute truth.

Printed in the United States of America
Cover and Interior design: 1106 Design

To Marty, and to women and their children.

TABLE OF CONTENTS

ACKNOWLEDGMENTS

In an essay I wrote during my graduate work for Dr. Letty Russell and J. Shannon Clarkson, I stated, "I am still ignorant because of my inability to read the texts in their original language. I am grateful to theologians like Phyllis Trible who can read the texts in their original language and present the information in a form I can use." Letty wrote in the margin of my essay, "Even if you could read Hebrew, you would need other interpretations to assist in interpretation—we all need another's help."

I am grateful to Letty and Shannon for mothering me through my Doctor of Ministry program.

In 1995, I was lucky enough to take a class from Sister Miriam Therese Winter at the Graduate Theological Union. She wrote three of the required texts for the class: *Woman Wisdom: A Feminist Lectionary and Psalter Women of the Hebrew Scriptures: Part One, Woman Witness: A Feminist Lectionary and Psalter Women of the Hebrew Scriptures: Part Two* and *Woman Word: A Feminist Lectionary and Psalter Women of the New Testament.* In her three-volume work she found, named and celebrated in song, prayer, psalm and reflection, all the women of the Bible. I have read and re-read these books and relished Sister

Miriam's woman-centered words. The books have been invaluable to me as I searched out the stories of the women in the genealogy of Jesus, his family, friends, public life, parables and the women of the first-century church.

I wish to thank my neighbors Jack and Marijean Hawks for their insight and support, and my dentist, Dr. Robert McLachlan, for his encouragement and humor. He always makes me smile, and he is smarter than he looks.

Special thanks to my husband, Marty, who encouraged me throughout the writing process. I deeply appreciate my sisters Hilary and Sonya; they would stop what they were doing whenever I called and listen as I read to them what I had just written. Sonya always said, "Interesting," and Hilary always said, "I can't wait to read it."

I am indebted to my friend Hilary Christiansen. She grew up without church or Bible and as such was totally unfamiliar with the biblical stories. She enthusiastically read and critiqued my work. She was instrumental in drawing attention to the need for background information about these biblical women. Additionally, many thanks to Nancy Corran, who graciously offered her theological knowledge and insights although we had never met. Both of these women came into my life at exactly the moment I needed their expertise. Finally, thanks to publishers Cathy and Bradley Winch, who would say, "How usual."

INTRODUCTION

For just as the body without spirit is dead,
so faith without works is dead.
—JAMES 2:26

My work is writing this book. No matter what else I do, I must write this book. My sense of call is overwhelming. As a child in Sunday school, I always wondered *Where are the women in these Bible stories?* And, *Why are they all prostitutes, virgins or mothers?* It was this question, among others, which prompted me to study religion. I began to learn that the stories of women in the Bible had been written by men and were communicated to me through the interpretations of male scholars and ministers. I perceived there was more than one way to interpret the stories of women and men in the Bible. I earned my Bachelor of Arts degree in Religion at Chapman College and my Master of Arts degree in Religion at Liberty University. It was there that the full force of the subject matter of this book hit me. Later I received a Doctor of Ministry in International Feminist Theology at San Francisco Theological Seminary.

I write this book because the reach for wisdom by Eve in Genesis has been interpreted as the reason for the evil in the world and because I am exhausted with hearing Mary Magdalene called a prostitute even though there is no evidence for this in the Bible. I am fed up with traditional interpretations of Scripture. I believe there are different ways to interpret the Scriptures, interpretations from the perspective of a twenty-first century woman, a perspective vastly different from that of a first-, second- or any other -century man. I write this book because my God, my Creator, in whose image and likeness I am created, has called me to write it.

There are some who might argue that my sense of call is subjective and that it ignores biblical criteria for ministry and teaching. I believe there is ample biblical evidence to demonstrate the call of women and men to ministry, teaching and leadership. I believe Bible study can be more than traditional Bible study. Bible study can include a clear understanding of historical setting, geographical location of events, intention and audience of the author, as well as the meaning of the text to a modern reader.

I am a cradle Christian. I started my faith life as a Protestant and later became a Roman Catholic. Now I am a member of an Independent Catholic Community. As a woman, my call is not fully recognized by the Roman Catholic Church and many Protestant denominations, including the one that sponsors Liberty University.

God is credited in Isaiah 1:17–18 with saying, "Learn to do good. Make justice your aim: redress the wronged, hear the orphan's plea, defend the widow. Come now, let us set things right." (NAB) I write this book to set right the institutionalized response to my call and that of many other women.

I believe in a good and just God who does not repress or discriminate. The stories of the people in the genealogy and life of Jesus are bursting with examples of God's goodness and justice toward women and men. I believe in a Jesus who attempted to model God's loving, inclusive relationship with creation. To paraphrase 1 Peter 1:17, my creator judges me impartially, according to my deeds. This is my understanding of God and my relationship with and experience of God. I base my understanding on an uncensored awareness of who God has called me to be.

I believe I am, as all women are, created in the image and likeness of God. To summarize Genesis 1:27, God created humans in God's image, in the divine image God created them male and female. In her book *Women's Bodies, Women's Wisdom,* Dr. Christiane Northrup asks this question: "Do you understand how inherited cultural attitudes toward our female physiological processes such as menstruation and menopause have contributed to the illness suffered by our female bodies?"[1] I am appalled that girls are not taught to celebrate their marvelous bodies which were created in the image and likeness of God, bodies endowed with the God-like ability to produce life. God must, in some magnificent way, be female, as I and all women created in the image and likeness of God reflect. "The birthing image of God is prevalent in Scripture, the one who brings forth life."[2] In Isaiah 42:14, God is said to compare God's self with a woman in labor.

Creation has been ordered marvelously! The creation story in Genesis 1:8 introduces the cycle of evening and morning. We experience cycles all around us. Does it make sense that the cycles of women's bodies are anything less than marvelous? Shortly after the creation of male and female in Genesis 1:27, God looks over the creation and pronounces it "very good." One has to look past the interpretations handed down to us by men who, not only in Christianity but history in general, have been the creators and generators of knowledge.

How did we lose the image of the divine feminine? Why, in a faith where both genders are created in the image and likeness of the Creator, are women treated as less than the image and likeness of God, less

---

1 Christiane Northrup, *Women's Bodies, Women's Wisdom: Creating Physical and Emotional Health and Healing* (New York: Bantam Books, 1998), 590.

2 Nancy Corran, written message to author, July 2011.

than full human beings, less than full participants in the worship of God? The God who has called me is not a God of dominance and repression but one of liberation and release.

Chicano historian Jesus Chararra once said, "As long as you do not write your own story and elaborate your own knowledge, you will always be a slave to another's thoughts."[3] I am called to the freedom of writing my own story and elaborating my own knowledge. I write to know what I think, to examine my set of unexamined beliefs. It is essential to understand why we believe what we believe, whether it is about our faith or who we believe ourselves to be. By identifying what we believe about God's relationship to creation, we can discover what we believe about our relationship to God and our relationship to God's creation.

I also write to understand the people in the Bible and their relationships. Not as biblical heroes and sheroes but as people. Why did Sarah marry her half-brother, or Rebekah, Leah and Rachel their cousins? Why was it acceptable for Abraham and Jacob to have intercourse with the slaves of their wives? How far did Sarah, Abraham and Hagar travel? Where are the women, and how are they important to the biblical stories? It is these and many other questions I want to answer.

The original subtitle of this work was, "Why Do We Believe What We Believe?" The question was meant to encourage readers to examine their unexamined beliefs. We believe what we believe because before 1971, men for the most part, were the only gender permitted to produce knowledge, interpret Scripture or even attend many colleges and universities. This sexism is still being practiced today in the name of religion. As I write this, CNN Headline News is reporting the burning of a woman and some girls in Pakistan. The perpetrators used water pistols to spray acid on a female teacher and

---

3 I believe this quote came from the *Christian Century*. I have not been able to find the exact publication.

the female students with her. The men responsible for this atrocity reported they committed this act of violence "because the girls were going to school."

We are naturally horrified by a report of such extremism, but there was a time in the United States when girls were not allowed to get an education. In 1962, when I was nine years old, Yale University was considering admitting women as undergraduates for the same serious education it gave men. A male psychiatric consultant advised Yale, "The primary road to identity for a woman is marriage and motherhood, serious educational interests or commitments which may cause conflicts in her role as wife and mother should be postponed until the childbearing years are over."[4] Dr. Christiane Northrup reminds us in *Women's Bodies, Women's Wisdom,* "We've all inherited the belief that a woman cannot develop herself fully without simultaneously sacrificing her ability to serve her family."[5] The Yale University Library web site, *Milestones in the Education of Women,* reports that the first class of female undergraduates graduated in 1973. One of the classes they might have taken was titled, "Women in a Male Society."[6] The site also reports that in 1783, Lucinda Foot, age twelve, was examined by President Ezra Stiles. He found, "That were it not for her sex, she would be considered fit to admit as a student in the freshman class at Yale University."[7] Imagine the brilliant mind that must have resided in that twelve-year-old female body. How many brilliant minds have been wasted? How many unique understandings and teachings about the divine have been lost because of the gendered body in which that brilliant mind or unique understanding resided?

---

4 Betty Friedan, *The Feminine Mystique* (New York: W.W. Norton & Company, 1984), 365.

5 Northrup, 88.

6 Schiff.

7 Judith Schiff, "Milestones in the Education of Women at Yale," *Yale University,* April 6, 2011. http://www.yale.edu/oir/open/pdf_public_/WOO9_Enroll.Wom_Milestones .pdf.

We now think of a freshman as a first-year student of either gender at a high school or college, but the term originally meant men only. A four-year degree was named a bachelor's degree because it referred to "a young man in the first or probationary stage of knighthood; hence a man who was not married."[8] With this in mind, the male generic language behind *junior, senior* and *master* is blatant. Discrimination is discrimination. The question is how extensive is the discrimination. Is the objective to keep women out of school, out of the pulpit, secluded in the home or to use religious interpretations as an excuse to spray women with acid?

My sister's response to the original subtitle of this book was, "How do you know?" My answer, "Does it make sense?" Does it make sense that God is a racist? Does it make sense that God discriminates within any part of creation? Biblical justifications for discrimination against women are still used to deny women full access to many aspects of our faith traditions. As the Bible was used to justify slavery in the past, it is used today to justify discrimination against women.

Slavery existed in ancient civilizations. Slavery inhabited our own not-too-distant past, and its oppression continues today even if invisibly in the lives of black Americans and trafficked women and children. According to the website *religioustolerance.org*, Genesis 9:25–27 was a primary weapon used by slave owners to justify owning slaves. "The American slave owner felt he was carrying out God's plan by buying and using slaves."[9] The biblical text reads, "Cursed be Canaan; lowest of slaves shall he be to his brothers." He also said, "Blessed by the Lord my God be Shem; and let Canaan be his slave. May God make space for Japheth, and let him live in the tents of Shem; and let Canaan be his slave." (NRSV)

---

8 *New Webster's Dictionary of the English Language*, 2nd ed., s.v. "bachelor."

9 B. A. Robinson, "Supportive Passages from the Hebrew Bible (a.k.a. Old Testament), *Religious Tolerance*, July 29, 2010. http://www.religioustolerance.org.

On Sunday, November 14, 2010, the television program *Sunday Morning with Charles Osgood* aired a story about the integration of the William Frantz School in New Orleans, Louisiana. The story featured two women, Ruby Bridges, a black woman, and Pam Foreman, a white woman. As a child, Ruby Bridges had been selected to integrate the William Frantz School. In 1960 she courageously walked through the crowds of screaming white protesters who were opposed to integration. She was in first grade at the time. Pam Foreman attended the school as a child also. Pam Foreman's father, Lloyd Foreman, a Methodist minister, believed in integration. He walked his little daughter, Pam, to school every day through the hate-filled crowd protesting against integration. In the documentary footage of fifty years ago, a white woman holds the Bible up to the white minister and hits the book as she screams something at the minister and his daughter. Slavery and any biblical justification for slavery does not make sense in our twenty-first-century United States of America any more than discrimination against women makes sense.

As believers, it is important to examine why we believe the things we believe. Do we study the Bible to understand an ancient people writing about their experience of the creation and their relationship with their creator, a people heavily influenced by the civilizations surrounding them? Do we read the Bible to learn about a prescientific people trying to make sense of the world around them? Do we interpret the Bible to apply a set of Bronze Age rules to a twenty-first-century people? I have heard people question Muslim women who wear hijab and burqas. A burqa covers the body from head to toe with a small mesh at the eyes to see through. Why, they ask, do you continue to accept a style of dress that was dictated in the seventh century C.E.? Yet many Christian women accept an interpretation of their Scriptures done by male biblical writers through the centuries—interpretations which may not be relevant to the twenty-first century and may, in fact, represent the interpreter's bias against women and not what is best for women. Why do we believe what we believe? The simple answer is the stories have been handed down to us through interpretations that leave out some of the most interesting and vital information about biblical women.

For the most part, women in the Bible do not tell their own stories. The stories of the women in the Bible are told *about* them and are often interpreted in very derogatory ways. Many of these voiceless women do not have names. We do not know how the women in the Hebrew and Christian Scriptures felt about the circumstances of their lives. For example, how did Bathsheba feel when her first child died? We are told about David but not Bathsheba, but women know how she must have felt! What was it like for the young widow, Ruth, to leave all she had ever known and go to a new country with her mother-in-law? How brave and desperate the hemorrhaging woman who touched the fringe of Jesus' tunic must have been. How horrible her life must have been to take the terrible risk she did.

It is not my intention to rewrite the Bible but to reflect accurately the historical and biblical information presented in the Bible as I reconstruct these women's stories. In fact this undertaking is part of a long tradition called Midrash. Midrash is defined in the *New Webster's Dictionary of the English Language* as, "An explanation of the Old Testament; the body of traditional scriptural interpretation written between 500 B.C. and 1200 A.D."[10] Traditional scriptural interpretation written between 500 B.C. and 1200 A.D. was done exclusively by male rabbis. The first female rabbi was not ordained until December 25, 1935 in Germany.

Jo Milgrom, author of the book *Handmade Midrash,* describes it this way: "The term *midrash* describes both a method and a genre of literature in which imaginative interpretation discovers biblical meanings that are continually contemporary."[11] Jacob Neusner describes

---

10 *New Webster's Dictionary of the English Language,* 2nd ed., s.v. "Midrash."

11 Jo Milgrom, *Handmade Midrash: Workshops in Visual Theology. A Guide for Teachers, Rabbis, and Lay Leaders* (Philadelphia: The Jewish Publication Society, 1992), 3.

Midrash as, "Assuming the infinite meaningfulness of biblical text, the rabbis took passages that were sketchy or troubling and wrote them forward. They brought to the Bible their own questions and found answers that showed the eternal relevance of biblical truth."[12] Judith Plaskow uses these words to express Midrash: "imaginative, literary amplification, open-ended, simultaneously serious and playful."[13]

Using the technique of Midrash, with gratitude to the women and men who have written Midrash before, I am offering these silenced women's stories. Their stories are based on the biblical text and are translated into the woman's voice. Each woman's story is then illuminated in a section titled "Observations." These observations are based on research into geographical setting, cultural characteristics and social location. Additionally, these observations are made from a female understanding of circumstances that inform women's lives.

Following is an example taken from Matthew 1:18. The text says, "When his mother was betrothed to Joseph, but before they lived together, she was found with child through the Holy Spirit. Joseph her husband, since he was a righteous man, yet unwilling to expose her to shame, decided to divorce her quietly." (NAB) Deuteronomy 22:20–21 clearly states that the punishment for a woman who is not a virgin when she marries is death by stoning: "If, however, this charge is true, that evidence of the young woman's virginity was not found, then they shall bring the young woman out to the entrance of her father's house and the men of her town shall stone her to death, because she committed a disgraceful act in Israel by prostituting herself in her father's house. So you shall purge the evil from your midst." (NRSV) Joseph would have known that Mary would be stoned to death. Mary would have known as well. What if Mary, instead of

---

[12] Jacob Neusner, *History of Torah: Essays on Jewish Learning* (New York: Schocken Books, 1965), chapter 1; quoted in Judith Plaskow, *Standing Again at Sinai: Judaism from aFeminist Perspective* (San Francisco: Harper Collins, 1991), 53.

[13] Judith Plaskow, *Standing Again at Sinai: Judaism from a Feminist Perspective* (San Francisco: Harper Collins, 1991), 53.

the writer of the gospel of Matthew, told her own story? "When I was betrothed to Joseph, but before we lived together, I discovered I was pregnant. I had never been with a man. Joseph was a righteous man and kept our laws, but he did not want to expose me, so he decided to divorce me quietly. Our law clearly states that death by stoning is the punishment for a woman who marries and is not a virgin. I was terrified so I ran away to my Aunt Elizabeth's home! Could the Spirit of God protect me?" Mary's story takes on a different character when told from her perspective.

I would like to mention here that I am aware of the fact that there are many women in the world today who experience the same atrocities as biblical women. They are sold, expected to bear sons, controlled by male family members, forced into arranged marriages and more. I write from the perspective of a privileged, white, middle-class, U.S. citizen. I have not personally experienced these atrocities. In no way is my writing intended to disregard the realities of many women's lives today.

In several instances, references are made to laws found in Exodus, Leviticus, Numbers or Deuteronomy. These books appear later in the Bible than the stories of the women found in Genesis. These laws may or may not have applied to the lives of these women. The references are used to help the reader develop an understanding of situations these women may have faced. This analysis may differ from what we have been taught or, in some cases, not taught.

A note on dates: unless contained in a quote, the designation B.C.E. (Before Common Era) is substituted for B.C. (Before Christ). C.E. (Common Era) is substituted for A.D. (Anno Domini).

In chapter one, Sarah will tell us her story, including her reaction to the aborted sacrifice of her son. Sarah, the first matriarch in the genealogy of Jesus, is not listed in the genealogies found in Matthew 1:2–16 or Luke 3:23–38, but her husband is. Other husbands are listed in those genealogies but the names of their wives have not been recorded. There are four notable exceptions: Tamar, Rahab, Ruth, and Bathsheba. Bathsheba is in Matthew's genealogy, but her name is not recorded. She is called the wife of Uriah. No women are listed in Luke's genealogy.

In chapter two, the women in Sarah's family—Rebekah, Sarah's niece/daughter-in-law, Leah, Rebekah's niece/daughter-in-law, and Tamar—narrate their stories.

Those remarkable women who are named in the genealogy of Jesus describe their lives in chapter three. They are Rahab the harlot of Jericho, Ruth the Moabite, and Bathsheba the wife of Uriah the Hittite.

Mary, the mother of Jesus, his unnamed aunt, and Elizabeth speak in chapter four. The sisters of Jesus do not speak. They are not given voices or names by the biblical writers.

The women friends of Jesus who were among the disciples who ministered to and supported Jesus tell their stories in chapter five. The women were the first to witness and the first sent to proclaim the good news of the resurrection.

Chapter six encompasses the women Jesus touched in his public life as well as the first person to proclaim Jesus as Messiah to the gentiles. We also encounter the women who figured in the parables of Jesus.

In chapter seven, the women who were disciples, apostles and ministers in the early church tell their tales. We also look at some of the texts which are used to limit the full participation of women in many churches.

In chapter eight, Eve shares her experience. We also examine the writings of some of the men known as church fathers. The writings about women by these men can be very painful to read. The distressing attitudes these men had about women are not preached from the pulpit when the church fathers are remembered and praised, but what they had to say about women has had a profound effect on attitudes toward women in the church and in the larger society.

The euphemism "set in stone" is employed to denote concepts that cannot be changed. In Christianity, those concepts are biblical interpretations done over the centuries by male interpreters. Several years ago, there was a bumper sticker which read, "God said it, I believe it, that finishes it." But the question is, does God still reveal God's self to and through the created world? Elizabeth Rankin Geitz states in *Gender and the Nicene Creed,* "A correct understanding of orthodoxy arises from a correct understanding of the nature of God and God's relationship to the created world. Just as God revealed Godself to the Israelites, so God's self-revelation continues today."[14]

In shocked silence, I listened as a radio preacher told his listeners, "That's what we believe. I don't know why we believe it, but that's what we believe." That statement generated many questions for me. What do we believe about the Bible? Do we believe that every word in the Bible is factual? How do we explain contradictions? Was the Bible inspired by God? Who was inspired? Were the original authors inspired or the first scribe to copy it? Perhaps the interpreters commissioned by King James or the International Bible Society which sponsored the translation of *Today's New International Version* of the Bible were inspired?

Socrates is credited with having said, "An unexamined life is not worth living." For me, an unexamined faith is not worth living. How am I, a woman, to understand a "holy book" which is so obviously written by men for men? How am I, a woman, to interpret Ezekiel 18:5–7, which states, "If a man is righteous and does what is lawful and right—if he does not eat upon the mountains or lift up his eyes to the idols of the house of Israel, does not defile his neighbor's wife or approach a woman in her time of impurity . . ." How does this include women, how does this include me, except as a possession not to be defiled or an object not to be approached because of her God-given, natural bodily functions, which Ezekiel labels as impure?

[14] Elizabeth Rankin Geitz, *Gender and the Nicene Creed* (Harrisburg: Morehouse Publishing, 1995), 2–3.

Dr. Fred O. Francis, my New Testament professor at Chapman College, "encouraged students to arm themselves with opinions and perceptions of their own and create their own point of view."[15] I am sure there are some who will be uncomfortable with a woman interpreting Scripture. I am sure there are some who will object to men not being at the center of the biblical stories. But it is time for women to interpret the biblical text for themselves, for other women, for our daughters, and for the men who encourage them. We believe what we believe because that is the way our religion has been handed down to us, by the men who have been allowed to interpret it to us and for us. Women have fabulous minds. We can use them to interpret our Scriptures for the life-affirming purpose for which they were intended. I keep a quote in one of my Bibles. It says, "How can we know the mind of God, until we learn to use our own?" Faith cannot be damaged by truthful examination, and an unexamined faith is not worth living.

[15] The Panther Newspaper for Chapman College, author unknown, published in the mid 1970s.

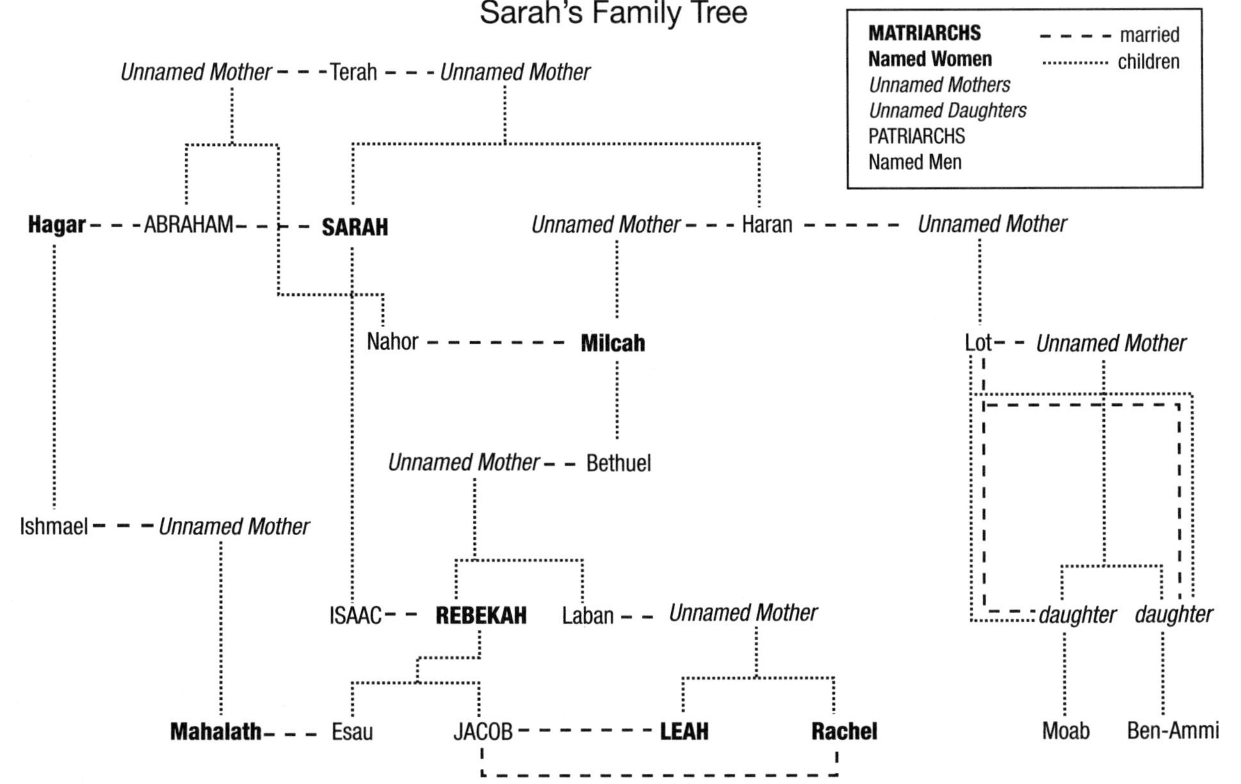
Sarah's Family Tree
MATRIARCHS
Named Women
Unnamed Mothers
Unnamed Daughters
PATRIARCHS
Named Men
married
children
Unnamed Mother
Terah
Unnamed Mother
Hagar
ABRAHAM
SARAH
Unnamed Mother
Haran
Unnamed Mother
Nahor
Milcah
Lot
Unnamed Mother
Unnamed Mother
Bethuel
Ishmael
Unnamed Mother
ISAAC
REBEKAH
Laban
Unnamed Mother
daughter
daughter
Mahalath
Esau
JACOB
LEAH
Rachel
Moab
Ben-Ammi

Chapter One

Sarah, the First Matriarch in the Genealogy of Jesus

The story of Abraham is important, so it is remembered and taught. The stories of Sarah, Hagar and the other women recorded in the Bible are equally important and interesting. There are no patriarchs without matriarchs. There are no church fathers without church mothers. It is time to celebrate the matriarchs and mothers of our faith. It is time to ask ourselves, "Why do we believe what we believe?"

In 1976, historian Laurel Thatcher Ulrich coined the phrase "Well-behaved women seldom make history." Although women have contributed significantly to every culture, their contributions, until recently, have rarely been recorded or remembered. Well-behaved women remain in the private sphere out of the public eye. "The Hebrew Bible mentions a total of 1,426 names, of which 1,315 are those of men. Thus, only 111 women's names appear, about 9 percent of the total."[1] Where are all the other women? Well-behaved women are those who do not cross the religious, social or cultural barriers. There must have been more than 111 women crossing those religious, social and cultural barriers.

The women who appear in the Hebrew Scriptures figured prominently in the stories of men. The women in Jesus' genealogy, family, circle of friends and public works whose names, voices and thoughts are recorded must have been remarkable. They were women who did not stay in the private sphere behind religious, social and cultural barriers. Their stories have been hidden or distorted by centuries of male-dominated interpretation. It is generally assumed that the biblical writers were male. What would the stories sound like if women told their own?

The stories of the women presented here may be unfamiliar to the reader. I suggest the reader have her/his favorite biblical translation handy. The chapter and verse for each woman's story is recorded before the re-creation to make finding each woman easier.

Women in the Genealogy of Jesus

In the genealogy of Jesus, found in Matthew 1:1–16, Tamar, Rahab, Ruth and Bathsheba are the four women named. However, we know the identities of at least some of the other women. The husbands of Sarah, Rebekah and Leah appear in the genealogy. Sarah's niece, Milcah, the grandmother of Rebekah, appears in the book of Genesis. King David's mother appears in the book of 1 Samuel 22:3–4, although her name is not recorded. In Matthew, Tamar, Rahab and Ruth are listed as the mothers of their sons, but Bathsheba is listed as the "the wife of Uriah." Ruth was a young widow. Tamar was a young woman widowed twice; Rahab was a prostitute; Bathsheba was a beautiful young woman who was spied upon and widowed by a powerful man.

1 Carol Newsom and Sharon H. Ringe, eds., *The Women's Bible Commentary* (Louisville: Westminster/John Knox Press 1992), 245.

All of these women were foreigners, that is, not Hebrews. Why do we believe what we believe about these women?

The status of women in the ancient societies in which we find the stories of Sarah, Milcah, Rebekah, Leah, Tamar, Rahab, Ruth, King David's mother and Bathsheba was vastly different from the status of many women in the twenty-first century. The laws concerning women are found primarily in the book of Leviticus but also in Exodus, Numbers and Deuteronomy. Girls and women were the property of their male family members. More pointedly, women's reproductive abilities were the property of the male members of their family. Daughters could be sold as slaves. Exodus 21:7 dictates the rights of a daughter sold into slavery by her father. The verse begins, "When a man sells his daughter as a slave, she shall not go out as male slaves do." (NRSV) The same chapter, verse 22, stipulates the fine to be paid to a husband if his pregnant wife is injured due to male violence and the violence causes a miscarriage. No fine is stipulated for the woman or her unborn child. Exodus 22:15–16 decrees that if a man rapes a girl, he must pay her father for the injury to his property, and the girl is required to marry her rapist. It is difficult, from our twenty-first-century perspective, to understand how or why a father would sell his daughter or force her to marry her rapist. It is anachronistic to project our ideas of marriage and family back onto the second millennium B.C.E., roughly four thousand years ago. Women had little status in the culture, aside from their roles as wife and mother, preferably the mother of sons. The good news for women in the stories of these foremothers of Jesus is that, despite these cultural constraints, these women left their mark in the Bible.

There is no transgression, aside from killing her own children, a woman can commit which society condemns more severely than a sexual transgression. Yet God is portrayed as using the sexuality, the reproductive ability and the character of women to accomplish God's plan. None of the women in Jesus' genealogy or life began their lives as powerful women. Each used her cultural knowledge, familial relationships, generativity and sexuality to transform her life into a catalyst in God's creative action in the world.

Where to Find Sarah's Story

Sarah's story begins in Genesis 11:24 with the birth of her father, Terah. Her story continues through Genesis 23:2. Sarah's story also contains the accounts of two other important biblical women, her slave, Hagar, and her niece, the wife of her nephew, Lot. She is also mentioned in Genesis 24:36, 67 and 25:10 as part of her daughter-in-law Rebekah's story. In Genesis 49:31, she is touched upon in a reference to the families' burial site. The prophet in Isaiah 51:2 calls her the mother of those who pursue righteousness and seek the Lord. In the Christian Scriptures, Romans 4:19 and Hebrews 11:11 allude to the barrenness of her womb. Hebrews 11:11 also lists her with the "Heroes of Faith." In Romans 9:9, the allusion is to Sarah as the mother of the children of the promise. First Peter 3:6 invokes Sarah as the model of submission, an interesting conclusion when contrasted with the times Abraham appears to agree quietly to Sarah's demands concerning Hagar and Ishmael.

Sarah Tells Her Story

> "Now that I am an old woman and my husband is an old man, am I to have sexual pleasure?" (Sarah, laughing to herself in Genesis 18:12)

I am Sarah. Although Abraham had other children, only through me and my son could the promise of God Almighty be fulfilled. My story is complicated. I was married to my half-brother, Abraham. We married kin within our own tribe. We have the same father but different mothers. Our family migrated from Ur in the year 1995[2] to Haran. We traveled along a trade route that followed the Euphrates River.

[2] That is, 1995 B.C.E.

Ur, the city of my birth, was a beautiful port city on the Euphrates. About three hundred thousand people lived in my city. It was the home of a prospering commercial society with a well-developed educational system. We had factories where women worked making fine spun fabrics. Artists and merchants settled in my city because a major trade route ran through Ur.

Our traveling party included our father, Terah, our brother, Nahor, and Lot and Milcah, the children of our brother, Haran. We took them with us because Haran died in Ur before our departure. Lot and Milcah also share the same father but different mothers. Milcah eventually married our brother Nahor.

We settled first in the trade center of Haran. Trade routes from the four corners of the earth meet in Haran. We lived there for many years and became very wealthy. In Haran, we accumulated possessions, herds and slaves. After the death of our father, there was nothing to hold us in Haran. Abraham spoke of an urge to travel further into the land of the Canaanites. Our nephew, Lot, and his wife went with us. We took all our herds, our possessions and our slaves, and eventually pitched our tents at Shechem, about thirty miles away from Haran.

Shechem, too, was a flourishing trade center. It was "the most important city and sanctuary in north central Palestine. It guarded the important east and west highway which passed between Mount Ebal and Mount Gerizim."[3] Shechem is located near the sacred oak at Moreh known as the oracle giver. There, in that sacred place, Abraham built an altar to God Almighty. This was the second time Abraham described his vision of God. His first vision had been our reason for leaving Haran. I am not sure when I began to realize that Abraham and I were destined for greatness. Abraham continually repeated that in his visions God Almighty told him we were to have children and would become a great nation.

---

[3] *The Oxford Annotated Bible: With Apocrypha*. Revised Standard Version. Herbert G. May and Bruce M. Metzger, editors. New York: Oxford University Press, 1965. Print.

Abraham was very restless. In due course, we moved our tents about twenty miles away to the sacred site between Bethel and Ai. Abraham built another altar. He called on God Almighty but did not receive a vision. We continued to travel toward the Negeb but, because of a famine in the land, we went down to Egypt.

Abraham broke my heart in Egypt. My beauty was highly prized, and Abraham begged me to say that I was his sister. We did not mention, however, that I was also his wife. Pharaoh heard of my great beauty and had me taken into his harem. Abraham was afraid for his own safety, taking no consideration of how I might feel about the violation of my body in Pharaoh's harem. Abraham's actions were cowardly and indefensible.

God Almighty was with me and caused severe plagues to strike Pharaoh and his household. Because of the plagues, Pharaoh returned me to my tent. He was very angry with Abraham and questioned him about his lies. In the end, Pharaoh's men escorted us out of Egypt with more animals and slaves than we had when we arrived.

This was the first time I realized that God Almighty was with me and that the promises Abraham talked about were for me, also. When I was taken into the harem, I was sure I would die there. We returned at length to the sacred site between Bethel and Ai where Abraham had built an altar.

Our nephew, Lot, was nearly as rich as we were. The land could not sustain all that we possessed, especially our combined herds. There was friction between the slaves who took care of our herds and the slaves who cared for the herds of Lot. Lot decided to move his household to the Jordan Valley. It was a beautiful region with plenty of water, like the garden of God. After Lot left, we moved our tents again, this time to the sacred oaks of Mamre near Hebron.

Things went very badly for Lot and his family in the Jordan Valley. There was a war between the kings of the region. Lot, his family, and all he possessed were taken captive. When Abraham found out, he took three hundred and eighteen of our male slaves who had been trained for war and went to rescue Lot. The campaign was successful. Abraham rescued Lot and the women who were taken captive with him.

Lot was greatly influenced by the people of the city in which he lived. He had two beautiful daughters. Both were to be married within the year. One evening, Lot received two passing strangers into his home. Lot's wife was a wonderful cook. People from far and wide knew of her cooking. Everything she made was seasoned to perfection. Lot loved showing off her great cooking and taking the credit for himself. When the men of the city learned there were visitors in Lot's home, they came banging on Lot's door, demanding that Lot send the visitors out to them. They were a vile group of men and had every intention of raping the visitors. Lot, instead, offered his beautiful daughters to the men and said they could do whatever they wanted to the girls. Thank God, the visitors were of higher moral fiber than Lot. They protected the girls, protected their mother, and protected Lot.

The next morning, Lot's family and the strangers escaped from the city. It would not have been a safe place for any of them to stay. The men of the city had been denied the chance to rape the visitors. They told Lot that he was in for worse than they had planned for the visitors. It was very lucky that they left when they did. There was a great earthquake in the Jordan Valley and a holocaust of fire. We could see the smoke rising in the valley from a place a short distance from where our tents were pitched. It was rumored that Sodom was destroyed because of the sexual sins of the men of the city. I pondered why the women and children had to suffer the same fate. Lot's daughters told me later that their mother had been furious with Lot! She said to him, "How dare you offer my daughters, the pearls of my heart, to that mob?" Lot's wife was killed in their escape. Many strange stories surrounded her death. The one most repeated was that she had been turned into one of the many pillars of salt near the Salt Sea, an idea which her daughters and I found ridiculous! She was, indeed, a pillar of strength in our family and the salt of the earth. Life seemed to have more flavor when she was around.

Abraham was convinced that God Almighty had appeared to him at the altars he built near the sacred sites of Mamre and Shechem. He was also confident that God Almighty promised us children who would inherit the land where we were living. He said the reason we left Ur was to take over the land. My recollection was that we left Ur at our father's urging. But Abraham was insistent.

I was not able to get pregnant so in desperation I gave my slave Hagar to Abraham in the hope that he would get her pregnant. Any child born of that union was a member of my household and my child. I was not to know until later what a huge mistake this would prove to be.

As I hoped, Hagar became pregnant. She did not seem to understand that the child she was carrying was mine. She began to show contempt toward me. I believe she thought she would take my place in my household because she was pregnant with Abraham's child. I said to Abraham, "The wrong done to me is your fault! I consented to let you go into my slave so that I could have a child by her, and now she acts as if the child is not mine. May God Almighty judge between you and me!" Hagar was my slave so it was in my power to do with her and the child as I saw fit. I demoted her from her position as my servant and disowned the child. Now the child would belong to her and Abraham, but it would not have the status of being mine. When Hagar found this out, she ran away.

She was gone a couple of weeks. She said she got as far as the oasis at Kadesh-barnea on the edge of the Negeb, a journey of approximately one-hundred thirty miles round-trip. When she returned, her attitude toward me was little changed. She claimed to have received a vision from God Almighty, like the vision Abraham claimed. She declared God Almighty told her that her offspring would be greatly multiplied. How many times had I heard Abraham say the same thing about our offspring? She said God told her to name her son Ishmael. She was even so bold as to claim that she named God! She called God El-Roi, the God who sees me. When her son was born, they named him Ishmael. He was a wild ass of a child, defiant, with his hand against everyone.

Shortly after Ishmael was born, Abraham had another vision of God Almighty. Abraham said in his vision God Almighty promised once again that I was going to have a child. Abraham did not believe his vision and fell on his face and laughed. He was very fond of his son, Ishmael, and begged God Almighty to recognize Ishmael as the heir of the Promise. My role in the Promise remained unchanged. It was at this point that Abraham changed our names. We were Abram and Sarai until that moment. Abram changed his name to Abraham and mine to Sarah, because he said our new names symbolized the descendants that were to come from our union.

He then did something very strange. He circumcised himself, Ishmael, and all of our male slaves, in fact, every male member of our household. The howling and crying of the men was deafening. The Egyptians practiced circumcision as did the Moabites, Ammonites and the Edomites, but the Canaanites, among whom we were living, did not. I believed it was the influence of Hagar, but Abraham claimed it was to be the sign of the covenant with God Almighty.

While our tents were at the sacred oaks of Mamre, three strangers came to Abraham's tent. Abraham seemed to know them, but I did not recognize them. He scurried around bringing water to wash their feet. He had a servant kill and cook a young calf, which he served to the strangers with milk and curds, a clear violation of our dietary laws. He asked me to make three cakes, but he did not serve them to the men. I thought it was strange that he would ask me to make cakes because making cakes was an act of worship to the Goddess Astarte of the Canaanite people, among whom we were living. I could hear the conversation from the door of my tent. There was something different, special about these men. They were talking about me. They asked Abraham where I was. One of the men talked about the child I was going to have. Abraham had talked about our child before, but this was the first time I had heard a stranger talk about my child.

I had not had a period for a long time so I laughed at the idea. The stranger took offense at my laughter. Odd—Abraham had fallen on his face and laughed the last time he had a vision about my having a child, and this stranger finds my laughter offensive?

Abraham was agitated so we moved our tents from Mamre again. I thought Abraham had learned his lesson from my experience with Pharaoh, but he had not. Abimelech, king of Gerar, took me into his harem, because Abraham told him I was his sister. I guess I had not learned my lesson either because I went along with Abraham. God Almighty was with me again. Abimelech had a dream in which God told him he was a dead man because of me.

The king called on Abraham in the morning and asked him, "What were you thinking that you lied to me?" Abraham admitted that he had lied and had persuaded me to do so on more than one occasion. He told the king he was afraid there was no fear of God in that place and that he would be killed. He was not thinking of my well-being, only his own safety. The king sent us on our way with more sheep, more oxen, and more slaves. He also gave us a thousand pieces of silver, to persuade everyone to overlook the injury done to me. Shortly after my encounter with king Abimelech, I discovered I was pregnant. That's when the laughter really began. Everyone who heard of my pregnancy was overjoyed for me. When my son was born, we named him Isaac. Isaac means, "He laughs." (RSV) When my son was eight days old, his father circumcised him.

When Isaac was weaned, I had finally had enough of Hagar and her wild ass of a son. Ishmael was fourteen years old. I did not want Ishmael's behavior to influence my son. He acted as if he were still a child, and Abraham and Hagar treated him that way. I demanded that Hagar and her son leave our household. Abraham did not want them to go, but God Almighty was with me. The next morning Abraham gave Hagar and Ishmael food and water and sent them to Beer-Sheba, about twenty-five miles away. Abraham followed them shortly. He planted a tamarisk tree and settled there. He made an agreement with King Abimelech concerning a well. Isaac and I remained in Hebron.

I thought my son and I had nothing to fear from Abraham. But, Abraham took my son and two of his servants on a journey. I had no way of knowing Abraham's intention on this journey was to sacrifice my boy. Thankfully, God Almighty was always with me and my son. Abraham had a change of heart and sacrificed a ram instead. The story Isaac told me on his return to my tent made me sick unto death. Isaac said they traveled for three days to Mt. Moriah. When they got there, Abraham was acting very strangely and made Isaac carry the wood for a burnt offering while the servants waited behind. Isaac told me he was terrified when he realized they had everything for the burnt offering except the sacrifice. He asked his father what they were going to offer and Abraham told him God would supply the sacrifice. Abraham was at the point of slaughtering my son when he saw a ram caught by its horns. Thank God Abraham released my son and slaughtered the ram. Isaac said his father kept wailing, "My son, my *only* son," but Isaac was *my only* son! Abraham had his first born, Ishmael. I could not endure the knowledge that Abraham had come so close to killing my child.

Observations on Sarah's Story

The story of Sarah and Abraham is placed in the Bronze Age, more than four thousand years ago. Abraham explains their relationship as siblings and spouses to King Abimelech in Genesis 20:12, "Besides, she is indeed my sister, the daughter of my father but not the daughter of my mother; and she became my wife." (NRSV) Other family members were married to each other. Sarah's half brother, Nahor, married their niece Milcah. Sarah's son Isaac married his cousin, Rebekah, and the twin sons of Isaac and Rebekah each married their cousins. Esau married the daughter of Ishmael, and Jacob married the two daughters of Laban, Leah and Rachel.

Ur, Haran and Shechem were large cities. Haran is the name of a city and also the name of Sarah and Abraham's brother. Likewise, the city in which Rebekah, the future wife of Isaac, lived is named for another brother of Sarah and Abraham, Nahor. The namesake of Shechem appears in the story of Leah and her children. Ur was an ancient Sumerian City in southern Mesopotamia.

The biblical stories of Sarah and Abraham did not develop in a vacuum, nor did they appear fully formed as we read them today. They have behind them the power of an oral tradition of an ancient people. The people Sarah and Abraham encountered had their own religion. The land through which they traveled had its own sacred sites. The places where Sarah and Abraham settled, near Shechem at the oak of Moreh or the oak of Mamre at Hebron, were sacred to the people who lived in the area. The sacred sites, where Abraham built his altars to God Almighty, did not become sacred because Abraham built an altar there; the site was already considered sacred to the Canaanites who lived in the land. In Genesis 12:6, Sarah and Abraham go to the sacred site at Shechem, which was known as a sacred tree, an oracle giver. Likewise, in 13:18 and 18:1, Sarah and Abraham pitch their tents by sacred oaks or terebinth. In 13:18 Abraham builds an altar to the Lord at the site, and in 18:1 the three heavenly guests visit that site. Ironically, this is the same site that the Israelites are commanded to destroy in Deuteronomy 11:30–12:3.

Although Milcah does not tell her story here, she was, by virtue of being the grandmother of Rebekah, an ancestor of Jesus. All we know about her are the names of some of her family members and that she had eight children. "Her relationship to Sarah and Abraham is complex. She was the daughter of one of their two brothers and the wife of the other one."[4] God is known by many names in the Hebrew Bible. In Exodus 6:2–3, God says to Moses, "I am the Lord. I appeared

[4] Miriam Therese Winter, *Woman Wisdom: A Feminist Lectionary and Psalter Women of the Hebrew Scriptures, Part One* (New York: Crossroad, 1993), 31.

to Abraham, Isaac, and Jacob as God Almighty, but my name is 'The Lord.' I did not make myself known to them." (NRSV) El Shaddai, which is translated as God Almighty, is the name for God used most often in Sarah's story. El is the name of the "Supreme and all-knowing god of the Phoenicians. As creator of the universe, he was known as 'father time.'"[5] The website *HebrewNames4God.com* says, "The word El comes from a root word meaning 'might, strength, power' and probably derives from the Ugaritic term for god."[6] "Shad means 'breast' in Hebrew."[7] *The New Oxford Annotated Bible* explains Genesis 17:1, where God is credited with saying, "I am God Almighty; walk before me and be blameless." "The phrase translated as *God Almighty* is variously understood as 'God the one of the Mountains,' 'God of the Shadday' [deities], or even 'God with Breasts.'" (NRSV) El Shaddai can be translated God with Breasts, an allusion to the feminine aspect of God. The website, *The Parent Company,* defines El Shaddai as "God Almighty. El points to the power of God Himself. Shaddai seems to be derived from another word meaning breast which implies that Shaddai signified one who nourishes, supplies and satisfies. It is God as El who helps, but it is God as Shaddai who abundantly blesses with all manner of blessings."[8] It is God, with breasts, who abundantly blesses with all manner of blessings, not an all-male God. Men may be said to have breasts, but there is no nourishment to be found in them. Some of the blessings which the Almighty promises in Genesis are blessings of the breast and blessings of the womb.

Pronouns do not make God a male any more than being called a "guy" as in, "Hey, you guys," makes me male. Hidden behind the male pronouns is a God who looks like me, the God in whose image

---

[5] Cynthia O'Neil, Peter Casterton and Catherine Headlam, eds., *Goddesses, Heroes and Shamans: The Young People's Guide to World Mythology* (New York: Scholastic, 1999), 69.

[6] John J. Parsons, "The Hebrew Names of God-EL," *Hebrew for Christians,* November 3, 2010. http:// www.hebrew4christians.com/Names_of_G-d/el.html.

[7] Parsons.

[8] "Names of God 6 (El-Shaddai)," *The Parent Company,* February 25, 2011. http://www.parentcompany.com/awareness_of_god/nog6.html.

and likeness women were created, as recorded in Genesis 1:27, a God who says, "I am El Shaddai," a God with breasts. Do I believe that God actually has genitalia which distinguish God as male or female? No! God is spirit. What I do believe is that, in some marvelous way, God is both male and female.

Amy Grant and Benny Hinn, among others, sing a song titled, "El Shaddai." On a YouTube video, Amy Grant introduces the song by saying that she has seen a lot of fads come and go, but God never changes. Yet in that one song, God is called by three different names: El Shaddai, El-Elyon, Adonai, and referenced as El-Roi, the God who sees me (the name given to God by Hagar, who is the *only* person to name God in the Bible). The name El-Elyon, "stressed God's strength, sovereignty and supremacy (Gen. 14:20; Ps. 9.2). Sometimes referred to in Scripture simply as Elyon (e.g., Num. 24:16)."[9] The name Adonai, meaning Lord, is used in substitution for the unpronounceable name of God, YHWH. As mentioned above, God changed God's name from El Shaddai to YHWH in Exodus 6:2, meaning "I am the Lord." God may not change but certainly seems to change the ways in which God reveals God's Self to humans. The song "El Shaddai" says, "Age to age, You're still the same by the power of the name El Shaddai." God with breasts.

Twice Abraham puts Sarah in danger by passing her off to powerful men as his sister. He does this out of fear for his own safety. He persuades Sarah to tell Pharaoh that she is his sister, and again he begs her to tell King Abimelech the same. Abimelech appears twice: First in Genesis 20:1–18 when Sarah is taken into the king's harem. The second appearance of Abimelech is in Genesis 21:22–34. Hagar, Ishmael and Abraham are living in Beer-Sheba. Sarah is not mentioned. Abraham and Abimelech make a covenant about a well Abraham has dug. It appears Sarah and Isaac stayed in Mamre.

---

9 Parsons.

The Bible says in Genesis 22:2 that God tells Abraham to take his only son, whom he loves, and offer him as a burnt offering, which Abraham attempts to do. But Isaac is not Abraham's only son; Isaac is Sarah's only son. Abraham had his first born son, Ishmael, by the slave Hagar. What was Sarah's reaction to Abraham's plan to sacrifice her son? It is shortly ofter Abraham and Isaac return from the aborted sacrifice that Sarah dies. Did the news that Abraham had intended to sacrifice her son give Sarah a heart attack?

Hagar and Lot's Nameless Wife

These women do not tell their stories. They are not in the genealogy of Jesus, but their stories are important.

Although Hagar and Ishmael are not in the genealogy of Jesus, they do figure prominently in the story of Sarah and her son, Isaac. If viewed through a twenty-first-century lens, they were treated abominably by Sarah and Abraham. Hagar is required to have intercourse with Abraham and produce a child. Eventually, she and her son are evicted from their home with Sarah and Abraham. If we have been taught about Hagar and Ishmael at all, we were most likely taught that when they were forced to leave the camp of Sarah and Abraham in Mamre, they wandered alone in the wilderness. Genesis 21:14 says, "So Abraham rose early in the morning and took bread and a skin of water, and gave it to Hagar, putting it on her shoulder, along with the child, and sent her away. And she departed, and wandered about in the wilderness of Beer-Sheba." (NRSV) We may also have been taught that when, in her despair, Hagar put her child under a bush to die, God intervened and showed her a spring from which to drink. Genesis 17:15 says that Abraham was eighty-six when Ishmael was born, and Genesis 21:5 notes that he was one hundred when Isaac was born. The child Hagar is wandering with would have been more than fourteen years old because Hagar and Ishmael are sent away after Isaac is weaned. Looking at the map and reading the text carefully,

I realized that the wilderness of Beer-Sheba where they wandered is about 25 miles from Mamre, where Sarah lived. Furthermore, there was a road between Beer-Sheba and Mamre. The journey from Mamre to Beer-Sheba, walking for five hours at three miles per hour, would have taken about two days. If we skip over the verses that give us some details about Hagar and her son, we find Abraham living in Beer-Sheba, planting a tamarisk tree and making a covenant with King Abimelech for a well. Where is Sarah? She appears to have stayed behind. After she demands that Hagar and her son be sent away, she does not appear in the story again until her death. She is buried in Mamre. Did Abraham leave Sarah in Mamre to follow Hagar and her son to Beer-Sheba? Genesis 21:11 says, "The matter was very distressing to Abraham on account of his son." (NRSV) Hagar is visited by God just as Abraham had been. She receives the same promise from God. Genesis 16:10 says, "The angel of the Lord also said to her, 'I will so greatly multiply your offspring that they cannot be counted for multitude.'" (NRSV) We can only guess what the relationship among the three of them was, but it does not appear from the text that Hagar wandered in Beer-Sheba by herself for long.

Ishmael continues in the story of Abraham and Isaac. In Genesis 25:9 we find Ishmael and Isaac burying their father. When Isaac's son, Esau, marries a third wife, she is one of Uncle Ishmael's daughters.

Contained in the story of Sarah is the perplexing punishment of Lot's nameless wife. Although Lot's wife is not in the genealogy of Jesus, her appearance in the story of Sarah demands a closer explanation. Why do we believe what we believe about Lot's wife?

Was she turned into a pillar of salt as a punishment for looking back? Was she turned into a pillar of salt to explain naturally occurring geographical land formations in the area? Was she turned into a pillar of salt as a literary device to prove the truth of the story of the destruction of Sodom and Gomorrah? Was she turned into a pillar of salt to divert the reader's attention from her husband's offer to let a mob of men rape her two daughters? The *Webster's New Collegiate*

Dictionary defines a pillar as "A firm, upright, insulated support, narrow compared to its height for a superstructure; more widely, any vertical support; also a shaft standing alone, as for a monument."[10] Firm, upright, supportive, monumental are all very positive, powerful images for women.

Salt, too, has many positive connotations. Jesus refers to the crowd that listens to him in Matthew 5:13 as the salt of the earth. Salt is widely used to bring out the flavors in food. Leviticus 2:13 states, "You shall not omit from your grain offerings the salt of the covenant with your God; with all your offerings you shall offer salt." (NRSV) The commentary for that verse in *The New Oxford Annotated Bible* states, "Salt of the covenant, salt as a preservative, symbolized the perpetuity of the covenant." (NRSV) In Numbers 18:19, Aaron and all his descendants, male and female, are given a covenant of salt. Second Chronicles 13:5 states, "Do you not know that the Lord God of Israel gave the kingship over Israel forever to David and his sons by a covenant of salt?" (NRSV) The commentary states, "Covenant of salt, the reference to 'salt' indicates that the kingship that has been covenanted to David will be enduring." (NRSV)

Instead of an interpretation of Lot's wife being punished for looking back, the interpretation of her story could be: Because of her experiences, she was transformed into a firm, supportive, powerful, monument to the covenant of God. She was the salt of the earth, bringing out the flavor in all she touched. The commentary on Genesis 19:26 says, "This text turns salt formations in the Dead Sea area into a testimony to the truth of the story, asserting that one of those formations was Lot's wife who disobediently looked back at the cities God was destroying." (NRSV)

Why is it necessary or even helpful to equate natural salt formations with the destruction of a woman? We are not told how Lot's wife felt about her husband offering her daughters to a mob of men to be raped,

---

10 *Webster's New Collegiate Dictionary,* 2nd ed., s.v. "pillar."

but we can imagine. If she did look back, perhaps her daughters were behind her and she was checking on their safety. Perhaps the story turns her into a pillar of salt to avert the reader's attention from her anger at her husband's willingness to offer her daughters to the mob of rapists. Or, perhaps she is punished to redirect our attention from Lot's abominable behavior regarding his family.

Lot does not seem to be of the highest moral fiber. Hospitality notwithstanding, what kind of man would offer his daughters to a mob to be raped? *The New Oxford Annotated Bible* goes to great length to justify Lot's actions, "As in the case of 18:1–8, the main issue here is hospitality to secretly divine visitors. Here, however, the sanctity of hospitality is threatened by the *men of the city* who wish to rape (know) the guests (cf. Judges 19:22–30). Though disapproval of male homosexual rape is assumed here, the primary point of this text is how this threat by the townspeople violates the value of hospitality (contrast 18:1–16). Hospitality is valued so strongly in this context that this text positively portrays Lot's offer of his virgin daughters in place of his guests. Though the text presupposes that a father would have extreme difficulty offering his daughters to such violence, Lot's virtue is demonstrated by his willingness to go to such length—and put his own body in danger (9vv.9–10)—to avoid violation of his guests." (NRSV)

The text calls male homosexual rape "wicked." But where is disapproval of the rape of young women assumed? The commentary says the threat was from *townspeople*, but the text says it was *men* who were the threat. When does the *Bible* mean men, when does it mean women, and when does it mean both? The commentary states that the text "positively portrays Lot's offer of his virgin daughters." Is there a way to positively portray the offer of daughters, virgin or otherwise, to a mob of men to be raped? No, there is no way to positively portray the offer of daughters to be raped!

Where does the text presuppose that a father would have difficulty offering his daughters to such violence? The text does not presuppose it, regardless of the commentary referenced above. The text says, "I beg you, my brothers, do not act so wickedly. Look, I have two daughters who have not known a man; let me bring them out to you, and do to them as you please; only do nothing to these men, for they have come under the shelter of my roof." (NRSV) Why were the daughters not shown the same consideration as passing strangers? Were the daughters not under the shelter of their father's roof? Lot's wife is said to have been punished for looking back. Why was there no punishment for offering one's daughters to a mob for rape?!

In verse 19:16, it is Lot who lingers in Sodom and has to be seized and taken outside the city. Why was there no punishment of Lot for disobeying? It is Lot who begs the visitors not to force him to flee to the hills where they have commanded him to go. He asks to be allowed to flee to the small city of Zoar. Why was there no punishment for arguing with the visitors, who are angels in disguise?

Shortly after the destruction of Sodom, however, Lot has left the city of Zoar because he is afraid to live there. He is said to be living with his daughters in a cave in those same hills to which he had begged not to go. The idea of Lot getting drunk and having intercourse with his daughters is attributed to the daughters. The older daughter is reported to say, "There is not a man on earth left to come to us." This cannot be true because after the destruction of Sodom and Gomorrah, they had fled to the city of Zoar. There must have been men in the city of Zoar. Genesis 19:30 states that Lot was afraid to stay in Zoar. Was it the women in the city that Lot was afraid of? Had they heard of Lot's offer of his daughters to a mob to be raped? Had they heard of the obliteration of his wife in the escape? How drunk would a man have to be not to know he was having sex with his daughters, which begs the question: if he were that drunk, could he even have sex?

The story of the destruction of Sodom and Gomorrah is the story of the destruction of innocent women and children who lived in those cities. In Genesis 18:22 the "Lord" promises that the cities will not be destroyed if ten righteous are found. Are we to assume that of the all the women and children in the city there were not ten righteous women? Or does the righteousness of women not count? The stories of Sarah, Hagar and Lot's wife and daughters are of the unimportance of women in the story of men. At least twice Sarah was placed in a situation which could have led to her rape, her child was nearly sacrificed, and her husband apparently abandoned her and her child near the end of her life. Sarah is invoked in First Peter to encourage women to accept the authority of their husbands but, in Sarah's story, she is the one who decides Abraham should sleep with Hagar. She is the one with the authority to send Hagar away the first time, and in Genesis 21:12, God is quoted as telling Abraham to do whatever Sarah tells him to do.

Lot's daughters were not shown the same consideration as the passing strangers. They were not safe under the shelter of their father's roof. Why do we believe what we believe about Sarah, Hagar and Lot's family? It is the stories of men that have been emphasized, not the stories of the women. If the stories of the women are taught, it is only to remind women not to disobey, as in the story of Lot's wife. Her daughter's stories represent the dispensability of women in the male agenda. Hagar's reproductive abilities were used by her powerful owners, and Sarah is given no voice in the decision to sacrifice her son. These women, however, were important as the story of God and God's people continued to unfold.

Chapter Two

WOMEN OF SARAH'S FAMILY

WHERE TO FIND REBEKAH'S STORY

Rebekah's story is recorded in Genesis 22:20–28:9. Rebekah's grandparents were Nahor, the brother of Sarah and Abraham, and Milcah, the niece of Sarah and Abraham by their brother, Haran. Rebekah married Isaac, the son of Sarah and Abraham. Like Sarah, her burial site is recorded in Genesis 49:31. Paul invokes Rebekah in Romans 9:9–11, to illustrate his argument for God's promise or election without regard for human action.

Rebekah Tells Her Story

"Let your curse be on me, my son, only obey my words and do what I have told you." (Rebekah's plea to her son Jacob, in response to his questions about the plan to deceive Isaac in Genesis 27:13)

I am Sarah's daughter-in-law, Rebekah. I never knew Sarah, but I heard many stories about her. I am from the same tribe as Sarah. My grandmother, Milcah, was Sarah's niece; my grandfather, Nahor, was her half-brother, and my great-grandfather was her brother. I married Isaac shortly after the death of Sarah, and we began our life together in her tent. Sarah was a great woman, and she had endured much as the wife of Abraham. When she died, Abraham bought a cave in Mamre in which to bury her. When Abraham died, it fell to my husband and my brother-in-law, Ishmael, to bury Abraham in the cave with Sarah. The six sons Abraham had by Keturah, after the death of Sarah, had been sent to the East country.

I lived with my mother, my brother Laban and my father, in a city named for my grandfather. My life changed dramatically one average evening when I went to the spring to get water as I always did. A servant, sent from Abraham, had arrived in the city of Nahor. I met the servant by chance when I went to the spring to draw water. He asked me for a drink which I gladly gave him, and then I watered his camels. For this he gave me two gold bracelets and a gold ring. He asked if there was any room in our home for his traveling party and their animals.

I ran back to my mother's house to tell her my story and show her the expensive gifts. My brother invited the servant and his companions into the house and provided food and water for his camels and his men. Little did I know what was in store for me! The servant told a fantastic tale of coming to Nahor to find a wife for the son of his master, Abraham, my uncle. He described how he had prayed to the God of Abraham that the woman to whom he said, "Please give me a little water from your jar," and who said to him, "drink, and I will draw for your camels also," would be the woman who would marry Abraham's son. That, as it turned out, was me. I was not astonished when my father and my brother, after hearing the story, said, "Take her and go." They did not consult me at all. Why would they? I was to be married into the tribe.

The servant and his men were tired and hungry. They ate, drank and spent the night. In the morning, my mother asked me if I was willing to go with the servant. She did not just say, "Take her and go," as my father had. I had thought about what to do all night and decided I would go. My mother begged that I stay with her for ten days. My brother supported our mother in her wishes. I knew that once I left I would never see my mother again. I decided to go quickly rather than spend the next ten days in the sadness of saying goodbye. My nurse and I left with the servant of Abraham.

Our journey took us the better part of a month. When I met Isaac, he was living in Kadesh-barne near the spring of Beer-la'hai-roi in the Negeb wilderness. This was an important place for my brother-in-law's family for it is where his mother went when she was pregnant and ran away from Sarah's camp. My brother-in-law lived in the Wilderness of Paran, a distance of about 50 miles from Kadesh-barne. The brothers remained close even with all the trouble between their mothers.

I think I fell in love with Isaac at first sight. He was walking in the field in the evening as we approached. I asked the servant who it was coming toward us. When I learned it was Isaac, I prepared myself to meet him while he talked to the servant. Isaac took me to his mother's tent and loved me. I believe I was a great comfort to Isaac after the death of his mother. She had been very sad when Abraham had moved from Mamre. Relations had been strained between Isaac and his father, after the aborted sacrifice. I think Isaac blamed Abraham for the death of his mother. Isaac said she had been sickened by the idea that Abraham would even consider sacrificing her son.

It took me many years to conceive. When I finally did, it was a terribly difficult pregnancy. I wanted to die. I prayed to God and received an oracle. I was to have twin sons. The younger would rule over the older, somewhat reminiscent of the relationship between Ishmael and Isaac. How true the oracle was to be I had no way of knowing.

The boys could not have been more different. My first born, Esau, had red hair which seemed to cover his entire body. My second born, Jacob, had very smooth skin. As they grew, Esau was the outdoors man. He liked to hunt and work with his father in the fields. Isaac loved him dearly. Jacob was a quiet child and liked to spend his time in the tent with me. He became a very good cook.

When he was a grown man, Esau married two Hittite women. They made life miserable for Isaac and me. Isaac and I were determined that Jacob would not marry a woman who was not a member of our tribe. I heard the stories of Abraham and Sarah's promise of children that would someday be a great nation. I believed that promise extended through my husband to our sons. I knew that Esau and his foreign wives were not the family through which the promise was to be fulfilled. I knew that Sarah had been unwavering in her belief that the promise was to be fulfilled through her son Isaac, Abraham's second born. I was determined that Isaac's second born would be the son of the promise. I remembered the oracle I had received before their birth. I knew that the younger son was destined to rule over the older so I devised a plan to trick Isaac into giving his blessing to Jacob. I had Jacob slaughter two young goats from our flocks. Poor Isaac was nearly blind. I sewed the goat skins so that they covered Jacob's arms and neck. If Isaac touched him, Jacob would feel like his brother. I also dressed Jacob in Esau's clothes so Jacob would smell like his brother. I made Isaac's favorite dish with the meat of the goats and had Jacob take it into his father. Isaac was fooled. He gave Jacob his blessing. When Isaac and Esau found out what we had done, they were furious. Esau began talking about killing his brother. I was afraid I would lose both my boys. It was better that Jacob leave than have my sons fight and one or both be killed. I told Jacob of Esau's plan to kill him. I wanted to send Jacob to my brother, Laban. Isaac agreed with me. We were both fed up with Esau's Hittite wives. Isaac called Jacob to him and sent him away to Laban with the command to find a wife from among my nieces. I never saw Jacob again.

Our betrayal had a profound effect on Esau. He realized that his Hittite wives were making our lives miserable. He went to his uncle, Ishmael, and asked for Mahalath for a wife. Mahalath, as Ishmael's daughter, was a cousin of Esau and Jacob.

Observations on Rebekah, Her Grandmother Milcah and Bethuel

Milcah is mentioned in Genesis 11:26–29; 22:20–24; 24:15, 24, 47. She is part of the genealogy of Jesus, because she is the grandmother of Rebekah. She was the daughter of Haran, who was the brother of Sarah and Abraham and the wife of Nahor, the other brother of Sarah and Abraham. The only other information we have about Milcah is that she had eight children. Of those eight children, one was named Bethuel. In Genesis 24:15, Rebekah states that she is the daughter of Bethuel, son of Milcah. However, Savina J. Teubal, in her book *Sarah the Priestess: The First Matriarch of Genesis,* offers a convincing argument that Bethuel is the daughter of Milcah and the mother—not the father—of Rebekah. "According to Philo, Bethuel, meaning 'daughter of God,' was the name given by the oracles to Wisdom (i.e. Sophia) and is a feminine name."[1] She further states, "I believe, however, that the name of Rebekah's father, Bethuel, was originally the name of Rebekah's mother, and that the change of the name from feminine to masculine was a redactor's clumsy attempt to introduce a father figure into Rebekah's matrifocal community."[2]

After Rebekah meets the servant at the well, she runs back to her mother's house, not her father's. Her mother is, sadly, not named, unless Bethuel as mentioned above is her mother's name. Because women were the property of the male members of the family (Rebekah's father and brother), Laban could say to the servant of Abraham, "Take her and go." It is Rebekah's mother who asks Rebekah if she is willing

[1] Savina J. Teubal, *Sarah the Priestess: The First Matriarch of Genesis* (Athens: Swallow Press/Ohio University Press, 1989), 171.

[2] Ibid., 62.

to go and asks the servant for more time with her. Rebekah appears to be a very courageous and decisive young woman.

In Genesis 24:62, Isaac is settled in Beer-lahai-roi in the Negeb. According to *The Westminster Historical Atlas of the Bible,* another name for Beer-lahai-roi is Kadesh-barnea. Beer-lahai-roi is on the border of the Negeb and the wilderness of Paran. Ishmael is said to live in the wilderness of Paran. Beer-lahai-roi is the same location where Hagar named God El-Roi in Genesis 16:14. Isaac is living in Beer-lahai-roi when he meets Rebekah. Isaac and Ishmael travel to Hebron (Mamre) to bury their father. We can only imagine the relationship between Ishmael and Isaac but they seem to have remained close geographically and, perhaps, even emotionally.

In Genesis 26, Isaac and Rebekah travel to Gerar during a famine. They have an encounter with King Abimelech very similar to the encounter Sarah and Abraham had with him. If Isaac knew about his parents' experience with the King, he did not learn any lesson from their mistake. But, King Abimelech did. Isaac placed Rebekah in the same kind of danger as Abraham had placed Sarah. Although Isaac lies to the King and claims that Rebekah is his sister, Abimelech does not take her into his harem. When the King sees Isaac fondling Rebekah, he confronts Isaac, learns the truth, and sends him away. There is no physical harm done to Rebekah. They move several times, finally settling in Beer-Sheba, the place where Hagar, Ishmael and Abraham were living when Sarah died.

Rebekah advances God's action in the world through deception, trickery and lies. Do her means justify the end? She had believed the oracle she received from God and used the power available to her.

Embedded in the story of Deborah (Judges 4:4–5:31), a prophet and a judge of Israel, is the story of Jael. Jael kills Sisera, a Canaanite general and an enemy of Israel. She receives him into her tent and offers him shelter, food and rest. When he falls asleep, she hammers a tent stake through his head. Jael, like Rebekah, appears to advance God's design through deception, trickery and lies, and in Jael's case, murder. Do her means justify the end? "Jael's action teaches us that a transgression performed with good intention is more meritorious than a commandment performed with no intent."[3]

Isaac, Abraham's second born, is to be the son of the promise, not his first born as patriarchal law required. Sarah takes steps to ensure that her son is the son of the promise when she has Hagar and Ishmael sent away. If Sarah had not acted in the best interest of her son, the promise would have passed from Abraham to Ishmael, not to Isaac. In Genesis 17:17, Abraham falls on his face and laughs when God reaffirms the promise that Sarah will have a child. He asks God if Ishmael can be the child of the promise.

Rebekah's second born son, Jacob, is to be the son of the promise, not his older brother Esau. To accomplish this, Rebekah acts decisively. She is willing to take a curse, if necessary, to ensure her second born son receives Isaac's blessing. We are told that Rebekah loved Jacob and that Esau's wives were an irritation to her. Aside from that, we are not told why Rebekah did what she did. The concerns and motivations of women were not significant to the male biblical writers. It is, however, fascinating and ironic that the deception of these women, Rebekah and Jael, further the male biblical writer's agenda to advance the actions of God in human history.

Where to Find Leah's Story

Leah was the supposedly unloved first wife of Jacob. She was not so unloved that her husband stayed out of her tent. She was the mother of six sons and a daughter. Leah's story is recorded in Genesis 29:1–35:29. She is mentioned again in Genesis 49:31, as Jacob explains to his sons that he wants to be buried with her, his parents and grandparents. She is also praised for her fruitfulness in Ruth 4:11.

---

3 Miriam Therese Winter, *Woman Witness: A Feminist Lectionary and Psalter Women of the Hebrew Scriptures, Part Two* (New York: Crossroad, 1992), 42.

Leah Tells Her Story

> "You must sleep with me tonight because I have hired you with my son's mandrakes." (Leah's pronouncement to her husband in Genesis 30:16)

My husband, Jacob, was my cousin, the son of my Aunt Rebekah. I never met Rebekah but I heard of her beauty, her kindness and, to some extent, her ruthlessness in getting what she wanted. I was given to Jacob by my father, Laban. He tricked Jacob into marrying me. Jacob's first love was my younger sister Rachel. Jacob worked seven years for our father so he could marry Rachel. On the night Jacob thought he was marrying Rachel, our father substituted me. Jacob, of course, realized it was me—and not Rachel—as soon as I removed my veils. Jacob didn't seem to be upset about the switch that night or for the next week we spent together, although he still wanted to marry Rachel. Jacob and I spent our wedding night together and I conceived. In the morning, Jacob and my father talked about my father's deception. Laban granted that Rachel could marry Jacob if Jacob agreed to seven more years of work for our father. He used some argument that in our country the younger daughter could not marry before the older daughter. Laban was a greedy man and used this as an excuse to get seven more years of work from Jacob. After our wedding week, Rachel became Jacob's wife as well.

Nine months later I gave birth to our first son. I named him Reuben. We were both very happy. My husband loved me, and I conceived our second son Simeon. We were joined again, and I gave birth to our third son Levi. I praised God for my husband and my three wonderful sons. Before long I discovered I was to have another child, and I named him Judah. Many of the people in the village knew that Rachel was Jacob's first love and they gossiped about my marriage. "Oh, she is not loved," they would say, or "The Lord has afflicted her with a bad marriage," or "She is hated by her husband." I didn't pay any attention to the gossip. I knew what happened between Jacob and me in my tent and I had four sons to prove it.

Rachel and I worked together along with the slaves our father had given us, Zilpah and Bilhah. At the harvest, my son Reuben found some mandrake root and brought it to me. Poor Rachel did not have an easy time getting pregnant. Mandrake is an aphrodisiac, and Rachel wanted some in the hopes that it would help her conceive. She was so miserable. I traded Rachel some of the root for another night with our husband and again I conceived a child. My husband honored me and I gave birth to a fifth son. I had six sons in all, not counting the two that my slave had for me. Finally, I gave birth to Dinah, my beautiful daughter. Sons are highly prized but every woman I know wants a daughter so she can pass on her stories and her mother's stories.

At last Rachel became pregnant! As much gossip as there was about my marriage, there was even more about Rachel. She had been looked on with reproach because she had not had a child. This had affected her relationship with Jacob. He had become very angry with Rachel when she had demanded that he give her a child. With the birth of Joseph, peace and joy were restored to our household.

One day, Jacob called Rachel and me into the field. He was very unhappy with our father. Laban was a greedy cheat, plain and simple. If that were not true, he would never have exchanged me for Rachel so that he could get seven more years of work out of Jacob. I remember the stories my grandmother used to tell about the day Abraham's servant came to ask our grandfather for Rebekah. She would laugh when she told the story of Laban running out to meet Abraham's servant after he saw the gold rings and bracelets the servant had given Rebekah.

Jacob was upset. Laban had agreed that the sheep and goats that were speckled or spotted would be Jacob's. Laban was continually dishonest with Jacob. He did not keep his word. Laban removed all the speckled and spotted animals from the herds and sent them a three days' journey away with our brothers. Laban was not a rich man before Jacob worked for him. Now he was much better off, thanks to Jacob's hard work.

Our brothers were cut from the same cloth as our father. They began complaining that Jacob had gained all his wealth from what belonged to our father. They forgot that our husband had served our father with all his strength for twenty years and that Laban had changed the agreement about wages ten times. Jacob wanted to leave Laban and return to his mother and father. We were in agreement with Jacob. Our father treated us like foreigners. He had sold us and was using any inheritance that was to come to us and our children to his own ends. Jacob had made us wealthy with flocks, camels, donkeys and male and female slaves. When Laban went to shear his sheep, we took all our possessions and left.

Laban showed up at our camp seven days later. All hell broke loose. Our father was so angry. He tried to make it sound like Rachel and I had not gone with our husband willingly, as if we were captives taken by force. He made a great show about the goodbye party he would have thrown and how he wanted to kiss us all farewell. I couldn't believe my ears! This was the man who had sold us to Jacob and treated us like foreigners, now claiming his love for his daughters and grandchildren. "They are my daughters, my children, my flocks!" he shouted. "All that you have is mine!"

Jacob's anger finally spilled over at Laban. "For twenty years I worked for you!" he shouted. "I took the loss of any of the animals that died, not you! You had very little when I came to you! You were blessed because of me! And now you charge me with being dishonest with you, after you changed my wages ten times and sent the animals you had promised to me away with your sons! I froze in the winter, and I burned in the summer, and at night I got no sleep! Now you follow me and accuse me of stealing, after twenty years of serving you! Let our relatives decide which of us are right."

I got really scared when Laban threatened Jacob with harm. But there was really nothing he could do. Jacob was right, and all our relatives were there as witnesses. So Laban and Jacob reached an agreement that Laban would not go past the spot where we were camped and Jacob would not return to Haran. In the morning, Laban left and we were on our way.

My sister can be a bit like Rebekah in that she knows how to get what she wants. Our father cherished the statues of our household gods. Rachel wanted them. When our father showed up ranting and raving about our leaving, he accused Jacob of stealing the statues. Jacob, of course, had no idea what Laban was talking about. He told Laban to search every tent and if he found them, the person who had the statues would be killed. My sister hid the statues under a camel saddle and she sat on the saddle. When my father entered her tent, she told him she was having her period and that she must remain seated. Laban got out of her tent so fast you would have thought he found a leper in there instead of his daughter. God forbid that Laban should be contaminated by a menstruating woman. We laughed at our father's reaction until we couldn't stand up.

Eventually we came to Peniel. Jacob sent messengers to his brother Esau in Edom about 120 miles away. Jacob had fled from Esau twenty years earlier when Esau had sworn an oath to kill him. Jacob and his mother Rebekah had played a trick on Esau and their father Isaac. Jacob was terrified that his brother had not forgotten his oath.

As the meeting with Esau grew near, it became obvious who was the most important to Jacob. He arranged our group so that Zilpah, Bilhah and their children were in the front, then my children and me, and finally Rachel and Joseph. I wanted to believe that he put Rachel behind me because Joseph was the youngest, but I was very hurt.

The brothers seemed to have a wonderful reunion with invitations and promises but Jacob had no intention of going to Edom with Esau. Even though he promised he would, we traveled about five more miles into Succoth and settled there.

Oh, how I wish we had stayed in Succoth, but we traveled on to the city of Shechem. Shechem, the son of Hamor, fell in love with my beautiful Dinah and forced himself on her. That was bad! In light of what happened after that, it was ironic and tragic that he did love her and wanted to marry her.

When Jacob's sons came in from the field, Hamor, the father of Shechem, was there. He asked Jacob and his sons if Shechem could marry Dinah. I was overjoyed for my daughter! She was to marry a man who truly loved her. After some of the experiences in my marriage, I could have hoped for nothing better for my daughter.

Her brothers were outraged—not for the sake of their sister, but because Shechem had violated their honor. Both Shechem and his father pleaded with Jacob and his sons. Shechem told them he would offer anything if he could marry Dinah. The boy truly loved her.

Jacob's sons can be very deceitful. I am not condoning what Shechem did, but what happened next was horror beyond my imagining. Jacob's sons convinced Shechem and his father that the only way they would allow Dinah to marry Shechem was if every man in the city were circumcised. Shechem's love for Dinah was so great that he somehow convinced every man to be circumcised. I believed in my heart that all would be well. Dinah had gone to live in the home of Shechem. But my own sons, Levi and Simeon, went into the city while the men were still in pain from the circumcision and killed every one of the men! I could not believe children I raised and loved were capable of such violence. They grabbed Dinah and brought her back to me. My poor Dinah—her heart was broken and there was no comforting her. Then the rest of Jacob's sons plundered the city. They took everything they could lay their hands on, including women and children. They used the excuse that they had done it to avenge their sister. But their deplorable behavior was about their honor, not their sister's. They had devastated her life, they had reduced my life to rubble, and they had completely destroyed the lives of the women and children of Shechem.

Jacob was very angry with Simeon and Levi. We moved to Bethel and Jacob changed his name to Israel. Jacob and his sons had become odious to the inhabitants of the land and they were abhorrent to me.

No one pursued us as we traveled. We did not stay long in Bethel. It was, after all, only about 20 miles from Shechem.

To add to my sorrow, my sister died in childbirth—she who had wanted children so desperately. My last, best hope, my first born Reuben, slept with Bilhah. Jacob cursed him for it. My Dinah would never be married now. She was not a virgin, so no man would want her for a wife. Two of my sons were murderers, the rest of Jacob's sons were plunderers, and now my sister was dead. It was too much for me to endure!

Observations on Leah's Story

Unfortunately, the traditional focus of Leah's story is on Jacob and Leah's sister, Rachel. It is on Jacob, of course, because he is the patriarch. Rachel is a focus because of her beauty, the place she held in her husband's heart and the method she used to trick their father when he came looking for the statues of his household gods. However, Rachel is not in the genealogy of Jesus. The line of descent travels from Leah through her son Judah and his daughter-in-law, Tamar.

The sisters are variously described in different biblical translations as, "Leah was dull-eyed, but Rachel was graceful and beautiful";[4] "The eyes of Leah had no luster, whereas Rachel had become beautiful in form and beautiful in countenance";[5] "Leah had lovely eyes but Rachel was well formed and beautiful";[6] "Leah's eyes were weak, but Rachel was beautiful and lovely";[7] "Leah was tender eyed, but Rachel was beautiful and well favored"; (KJV) and finally, "Leah's eyes were lovely, and Rachel was graceful and beautiful." (NRSV) The transla-

[4] *The New English Bible: With The Apocrypha.* New York: Cambridge University Press, 1971. Print.

[5] *New World Translation of the Holy Scriptures.* New World Bible Translation Committee. New York: Watchtower Bible and Tract Society of New York Inc., 1984. Print.

[6] *The New American Bible for Catholics: With Revised New Testament.* Confraternity of Christian Doctrine. Washington D.C.: World Catholic Press, 1986. Print.

[7] *The Holy Bible, Revised Standard Version.* Division of Christian Education of the National Council of the Churches of Christ in the United States of America. New York: Thomas Nelson & Sons, 1952. Print.

tor's note in *The New Oxford Annotated* states that the meaning for the word translated as "lovely" is uncertain. Why have interpreters and translators, over the decades, described Leah's eyes as either dull, lackluster, weak, tender and, at last, lovely?

Anita Diamant, in her novel *The Red Tent,* addresses the question of Leah's eyes this way, "Leah's vision was perfect. According to one of the more ridiculous fables embroidered around my family's history, she ruined her eyes by crying a river of tears over the prospect of marrying my uncle Esau. But my mother's eyes were not weak or sick or rheumy. The truth is her eyes made others weak and most people looked away rather than face them—one blue as lapis, the other green as Egyptian grass."[8]

What purpose does creating an antagonistic relationship between the sisters serve? In only one of the translations cited above, the most recent, is the word "and" instead of "but" used. "Leah's eyes were lovely and Rachel was graceful and beautiful." Why has the mother of six of the twelve tribes of Israel been criticized for her looks? Why has a word of uncertain meaning been translated using derogatory terminology? One might be tempted to say, "So what, why are Leah's eyes and Rachel's grace important to the story?" Apparently, then as now, women were appraised on the basis of their physical appearance. In her book *The Beauty Myth: How Images of Beauty Are Used Against Women,* Naomi Wolf calls the phenomenon, "The caste system based on beauty."[9] Are the sisters caught in a beauty caste system? What are we, as women, supposed to understand about ourselves based on the descriptions of Leah and Rachel's physical appearance?

The depiction of antagonism between the sisters is further exacerbated when Rachel is said to "envy" Leah and to have "wrestled" with her in a competition to produce children. It can be gleaned from the reading that Jacob loved Rachel. Yet, this did not keep him out

---

8 Anita Diamant, *The Red Tent* (New York: Picador USA. 1997), 11.

9 Naomi Wolf, *The Beauty Myth: How Images of Beauty Are Used Against Women* (New York: Anchor Books Doubleday 1992), 87.

of Leah's bed even after he fulfilled the required period of one week with her. Jacob must have cared for both women. When he is trying to decide whether or not to leave Laban, he talks to both sisters about what to do. They make the decision to leave as a family. When Laban catches up with them, Jacob tells Laban that he was afraid Laban would take both daughters away, not just Rachel. Finally, Jacob buries Leah in the tomb where Sarah, Rebekah, Abraham and Isaac are buried. His last instruction to his sons is to bury him in the cave with Leah, his parents and grandparents.

Although the sisters are portrayed as having an antagonistic relationship, they seem to be in control of who sleeps with Jacob. Leah exchanges some mandrake for a night with their husband and in Genesis 30:16 she tells him, "You must come in to me; for I have hired you with my son's mandrakes." (NRSV) Both sisters require Jacob to have intercourse with their slaves to produce children, much as Sarah did. The sisters are also in charge of naming their own children except in the case of Rachel's son, Benjamin. Jacob renames him after Rachel dies in childbirth.

We do not know if the sisters wanted to marry Jacob. Laban speaks of giving Rachel to Jacob. The text says that Laban "took" and "brought" Leah to Jacob. Both sisters complain that their father sold them. The text asks the readers to believe that Jacob did not know the difference between Leah and Rachel until the morning after the wedding. *The New Oxford Annotated Bible* says, "The exchange could be made because the bride was brought veiled to the bridegroom." (NRSV) This may be true but it hardly seems likely that she remained veiled all night. The text does say, "He went in to her." (NRSV) We do not know how Leah felt about being substituted for her younger sister. We do not know if Rachel loved Jacob. There is no reason to assume that the sisters had an antagonistic relationship except for the narrator's attempt to portray it as such.

We are not told what Leah's response to the sexual attack on her daughter was or the subsequent marriage arrangement. We can imagine Leah's reaction to the lying, murderous rampage of her sons Levi and Simeon, in Shechem. We can also picture her reaction when the other sons of Jacob destroyed the city and the lives of the women and children living there. As a woman, Leah likely had great compassion for the women whose husbands, sons, brothers and fathers were killed, women whose homes and city were destroyed and who, along with their remaining children, were taken captive.

How did Leah feel when her first born, Reuben, slept with Rachel's slave, a woman who, like herself, was a mother to Jacob's sons? They had worked together in the care of the family. Reuben was cursed by his father. That must have broken Leah's heart. We are told in Genesis 49:7 how Jacob felt but not how Leah felt. We are not told how she felt when she and her children were put in front of her sister in the company meeting Esau, or how she felt about the death of her sister.

Leah disappears from the narrative after the reunion of Esau and Jacob. The story of Joseph, found in Genesis 37, contains no mention of Leah. If she was alive, what were her feelings about the death, or supposed death of Joseph, her sister's first born? After the behavior of Simeon and Levi in Shechem, did she suspect they had something to do with his fate? Did Reuben, who did not want to kill his brother, confide in his mother about the fate of Joseph? Did she have any clue that Judah was capable of selling his own brother and breaking his aging father's heart? Did it fall to Leah to raise the last of Jacob's children? There are so many unanswered questions about the mother, the matriarch, of six of the twelve tribes of Israel and an ancestor of Jesus. Women's stories and experiences were trivial to the biblical narrators. Yet, women's lives and stories are at least half the fabric of a people's experience with their God.

The story of Leah is the story of a woman who makes the best life she can in the midst of the patriarchal narrative into which she is inserted. She, like so many women before and after her, uses her wits and the resources available to her to survive and, to some degree, thrive. The next young woman who marries two of Leah's grandchildren, and becomes pregnant by her son Judah, is just such a woman.

Where to Find Tamar's Story

Tamar's story interrupts the story of Jacob's sons and the selling into slavery of their brother Joseph. Tamar is a young woman trapped in a patriarchal marriage system and the law of Levirate marriage. She is the daughter-in-law of Leah's son, Judah. We are given no background information about her. Her story is found in Genesis 38:1–30. She, like Leah, is mentioned in verse four of the Book of Ruth. She is named in the genealogies recorded in First Chronicles 2 and in Matthew 1:1–17.

Tamar Tells Her Story

> "The man who owns this signet, cord and staff was the man who made me pregnant. Tell me, to whom do they belong?" (Tamar confronts her father-in-law as he is ordering her to be burned alive because she is pregnant in Genesis 38:25)

"I was very young when my father arranged my marriage. A Hebrew man named Judah wanted me for his oldest son. My husband's name was Er. He was an awful man and a worse husband. I cannot say I was sorry when he died. The rumor circulated after his death that he had offended God and that God took his life. Hebrew law requires that if a man dies and does not leave a male heir, this widow is required to marry the brother of her dead husband.

There I was. It was my responsibility to produce a son for Er so I was stuck with the other brother. His name was Onan. He was not much better than Er. I was required to have intercourse with him, which he didn't seem to mind, but he was having sex with me under false pretenses. Onan had no intention of producing an heir for his brother so he practiced birth control and would ejaculate on the ground whenever we had intercourse. He did not want me to produce a son for Er. If I produced a son, my son would inherit Judah's property and Onan did not want that. Onan died too. I suspect he had offended his God. He had ejaculated on the ground, wasted his seed, and broke the law by not producing an heir for his brother. There was one more brother but he was not yet thirteen.

Judah, my father-in-law, sent me back to my father's house to live a widow's life. As a widow, I had no status in society. I was neither a wife nor a mother. I was not a virgin so the prospects of my becoming a wife or mother were slim. I had no husband and no child. I had to wear widow's clothes so everyone who saw me would know I was a widow. I think Judah sent me back to my father because he didn't want to feed me and because he blamed me for the death of his two older sons.

Judah liked bragging about his family heritage. He would say, "I am Judah. My father was Jacob. My father wrestled with an angel, and the angel gave him a new name. His name is Israel. It means he who contends with divine and human beings and prevails." I wondered if, perhaps, Jacob had changed his name because of all the trouble in Shechem. "My grandfather was Isaac," he would proclaim, "and my great-grandfather was Abraham. Abraham was a friend of God and the father of the Hebrew religion." You would think with those great men in his family, he and his sons would have been better people. Judah never talked much about the women in his family, but my mother-in-law told me that Leah, Judah's mother, had a hard life. My mother-in-law said Leah had large, soft, beautiful eyes. Rebekah, Judah's grandmother, had twin sons, like I was to have by Judah. She was a woman who knew how to get what she wanted. She is said to have tricked her husband into giving the blessing of the first born to her youngest son, Jacob. Sarah, Judah's great-grandmother, was the matriarch of the family.

Years passed. I heard that my mother-in-law had died. I was sorry. She was a Canaanite, like me, and she was always kind to me. I also heard that my youngest brother-in-law, Shelah, was old enough to marry. Even though the law of Judah's people required that I marry Shelah, Judah had not sent word. I was finally fed up with the whole situation. My life had been stolen from me. Living as a widow in my father's house was only a half-life.

I decided to take my situation into my own hands. I had been at the mercy of my father-in-law and the laws of his people for too long. I heard that he was going to Timnah, about six miles from the town of Adullam where we live, to shear his sheep. I took off my widow's clothes and dressed myself as one of the sacred temple prostitutes of my religion. There is no shame for a Canaanite woman to act as a consecrated woman. I did not know if my plan would work. The Hebrew God is said to be very offended when the Hebrew people do anything to demonstrate a connection with another religion.

Judah was a lot like Er and Onan. I figured now that my mother-in-law was dead there would be nothing to stop him from doing anything he wanted. I heard some terrible stories about my father-in-law and his brothers. Rumors swirled that they sold their young brother to some traders because they were jealous of his relationship with their father. It was even said they stained their brother's clothes with goat's blood and made their poor old father believe his son had been killed by wild animals.

Sure enough, as soon as Judah spotted me, he walked right over and said, "Come, let me have sex with you." I really couldn't believe it was that easy. I thought I would have to proposition him. I asked him what he would pay me if I let him have intercourse with me. He said he would send a kid from his flock. I didn't trust him. He had not dealt honestly with me as a member of his family so I had no reason to believe he would deal righteously with a temple prostitute. I made him leave his seal, cord and staff. I really couldn't believe he would do that. Those were his most important forms of identification. He was not thinking with his head!

As soon as he had done his business, I changed back into my widow's dress, said a prayer to Ishtar, the fertility mother goddess of my religion, and a prayer to the Hebrew God. After all, it was the law of the Hebrew God I was trying to venerate.

I never got the kid he promised. Of course, he could not find the temple prostitute because there wasn't a temple prostitute, only me, taking my life back by the only means available.

A month passed. I was overjoyed to realize that I was pregnant. I did not tell anyone, but before long I didn't need to. I was huge.

Judah found out as I knew he would. I had no idea how much he really hated me. The usual punishment in the Hebrew religion for being pregnant when the father is unknown is stoning, but Judah decided to have me burned alive. The self-righteous hypocrite was very angry and indignant. He was yelling, "Bring the whore out. I'll burn her alive." He thought he had finally found a reason to get rid of me. I am so thankful that I had gotten his seal, cord and staff. On my way to be burned alive, I produced his things. I said to him, "You know you are the father of my child." You should have seen the look on his face. He was no longer yelling, "Burn the whore." He knew he was in the wrong. He admitted that I, a woman, was more righteous than he, because he did not give me his youngest son as the law required. He stayed away from me after that. It turned out I was pregnant with twin boys. I named them Perez and Zerah. They gave me seven grandsons. I took a huge risk, but my own well-being and my place in society were restored.

Observations on Tamar's Story

Rebekah tricked Isaac to ensure that her second born son would receive his father's blessing. Tamar tricked Judah to redeem her own life. Her actions ensure the promise of God to Sarah and Abraham. She must have had great insight into the character of Judah. *The King James Version of the Bible* that was presented to my father in 1941 calls this chapter, "Tamar deceives Judah." Judah would not have been deceived if he had not chosen to have sex with a prostitute. I might call this chapter, "Judah behaves shamefully to his daughter-in-law," or "Judah breaks the law by having sex with a temple prostitute" or even "Tamar takes control."[10]

Judah is said to settle near a certain Adullamite. The distance between Adullam, where Tamar and Judah lived, and Timnah, where Judah is going to shear his sheep, is approximately six miles. Tamar is said to be sitting somewhere in between. Judah believes she is a prostitute because she covered her face.

We do not know if Tamar wanted to be married to Er. The text says, "Judah got a wife named Tamar for his first-born Er." (NAB) We can assume that if Er was such an offensive human being that God is credited with putting him to death, he couldn't have been a very good husband.

The text says Onan did not want to produce offspring for his brother; yet he did not feel this so strongly that he refrained from having sexual relations with Tamar. The text says, "Whenever he had relations with his brother's widow, he wasted his seed on the ground to avoid contributing offspring for his brother." (NAB) The wasting or spilling of his seed on the ground so infuriated God that Onan's life was also taken.

In an obvious effort to diminish the significance of Onan's attempt at birth control, the commentary on this verse in the *New America Bible* offers a very interesting explanation for the reason for Onan's death. "It is primarily Onan's violation of this law, [that is, not producing an heir] rather than the means he used to circumvent it, [that is, ejaculating on the ground] that brought on him God's displeasure." (NAB) The *Webster New Collegiate Dictionary* defines an onanism as, "Uncompleted coition, masturbation."[11] Apparently God is not as offended with Judah's violation of the law (that is, not giving

10 Hilary Christiansen, written message to author, July 2011.

11 *Webster's New Collegiate Dictionary,* 2nd ed., s.v. "onanism."

Tamar to his youngest son to produce an heir for Er), because Judah is allowed to live. Perhaps, *it was the means* Onan used to circumvent the law (ejaculating on the ground) which offended God.

If the woman Judah propositioned had really been a prostitute, she would have been a temple prostitute, a consecrated woman, a sacred prostitute of the Canaanite fertility religion, and "a devotee of the mother-goddess Ishtar." (RSV) Judah's friend acknowledges this when he goes to find her to deliver her payment. When he cannot find her, he asks the men of the area where the temple prostitute is. He is informed that there is no prostitute there.

The New American Bible describes the women of the culture that Tamar is impersonating this way: "Temple prostitute: the Hebrew term *qedesha,* literally "consecrated woman," designates a woman who had ritual intercourse with men in pagan fertility rites." (NAB) Judah was a hypocrite. He knows that the woman he propositioned is consecrated in another faith. He knows what the law says about temple prostitutes. Deuteronomy 23:18 dictates that there are to be no temple prostitutes among the Israelites, male or female. He knows what the punishment for a Hebrew woman who "plays the harlot" would be but he has sex with her anyway. Judah did not fulfill the law by giving Tamar to his youngest son. He blamed her for the death of his first two sons, and he was still financially responsible for her. According to the website *womeninthebible.net*, "Tamar's actions were unorthodox by modern standards. But in a way she 'redeemed' Judah. She saved him from doing what was wrong, and was thus a pre-figure of Jesus, who was one of her descendants. Once again, God's plan continued to unfold through the unorthodox actions of a woman."[12]

Tamar must have been an important woman. Stories must have circulated about her courage. The blessing given to Boaz on the occasion of his marriage to Ruth invokes Leah, Rachel and Tamar

---

12 Elizabeth Fletcher, "Tamar and Judah: Her Story," *Women in the Bible,* June 29, 2011. http://www.womeninthebible.net/1.5.Tamar_Judah.htm.

as role models for the young woman who is coming into his home. Tamar is also mentioned by name in the list of the descendants of Judah, found in First Chronicles 2:4. In this case, she is called his daughter-in-law. And finally, she is listed in the genealogy of Jesus in Matthew 1:3. Her attestation in Scripture justifies her personal decision to take her life into her own hands in spite of the cultural restrictions placed on her actions.

Sarah and Abraham were half-brother and half-sister from the same tribe. Their son, Isaac, married his cousin, Rebekah, from the same tribe. The son of Rebekah and Isaac, Jacob (Israel) married his cousins, Leah and Rachel, from the same tribe. With the introduction of Tamar, the descendants of Sarah and Abraham begin to marry outside the tribe.

Chapter Three

Foreign Women in Jesus' Genealogy

Rahab the Harlot of Jericho, Ruth the Moabite and Bathsheba were not members of the twelve tribes of Israel. They prospered in spite of the very difficult circumstances of their lives. They were foremothers of Jesus.

Where to find Rahab's story

Rahab the Harlot was a brave and unconventional woman. Women, with few exceptions, do not choose prostitution because it is a profitable, respected, personally fulfilling career. Women choose prostitution because they have no other means to feed and provide shelter for themselves and their families, or their self-esteem has been so shattered they can see no way to support themselves but in degrading work. "Rahab also lived in the outer walls of the city which meant she was not a wealthy professional but a poor woman on the front line in case of war."[1] I believe Jesus understood this about prostitutes,

1 Nancy Corran, written message to the author, July 2011.

which is why he counted them among the people he spent time with and perhaps why he said in Matthew 21:32 that they would enter the realm of God before the chief priests and elders. Rahab's story is found in Joshua 2:1–6:25. She is also praised in the book of Hebrews 11:4–31 and James 3:25 as a champion of faith, justified by her works.

Rahab Tells Her Story

> "I have dealt kindly with you. Swear to me that you will spare the lives of my family and all who belong to me when you come to destroy my city." (Rahab pleading with the spies who are plotting the destruction of Jericho in Joshua 2:12–13)

I am Rahab, the prostitute of Jericho. My father was not able to take care of the family so the job fell to me at a very young age. I am a very resourceful woman. I was able to provide a home for my family in the walls of the city. I made fine linen from flax, and I rented out rooms in my home to strangers visiting my city. The travelers who rented my rooms talked of invaders going through the land. The reports were that their God was very powerful. It was said because of their God, the Red Sea dried up so they could pass. There were many rumors spinning around the region about what these warriors did to the kings of the Amorites. It was whispered that they utterly destroyed their cities, killing every man, woman and child.

Two men showed up at my house asking for a place to stay. I had never seen them before, and I had a feeling they were the invaders. My fears were confirmed when messengers from the King of Jericho came looking for them. I hid the invaders under the flax I was drying on the roof. I was very frightened for my family. If the rumors I heard were true, I had to do anything I could to save my loved ones. I admitted to the King's messengers that the men had been there, but I lied when I said they had left. I even told the King's messengers that, if they left quickly, they might catch the men.

When the city gates were shut, I thought it was safe. I went to the roof to talk to the invaders. I had to be very brave. I had a prophetic vision about these men. I told them I knew their God had given them the land and all the inhabitants of the land were afraid. I told them I believed their God was God of heaven above and earth below. I emphasized the help and kindness I had shown them. I asked them to repay that kindness and spare my family when they came to take the city. They told me if I gathered my entire family into my home and tied a scarlet cord on the window, they would not hurt anyone in the house as long as I kept their secret.

It was a horrible thing to see what happened to Jericho. The army of the Israelites marched around the city for six days. We were barricaded inside. On the seventh day, the Israelite army knocked down the walls of the city. They took all the silver, gold, bronze and iron. They destroyed everything. They killed every man, woman and child, even the infants. They also killed all the animals. It was horrible. When the men I helped came to the door, we were terrified. After the horrifying destruction we had seen, I was afraid they would not keep their word, but they did. They took my entire family to their camp. We dwell with them to this day. I have to believe I did the right thing to save my family. I wish I could have saved all the innocent people of my city.

Observations on Rahab the Harlot

Rahab was a prostitute. Tamar was forced to play the prostitute to protect herself and her future. Rahab, the prostitute, protected not only the spies sent from Joshua but, in doing so, her family.

Biblical commentaries can be more influential on our understanding of the lives of biblical women than the actual text. Sometimes the commentaries want to clean up the image of the women, and sometimes the commentaries want to cast women in a spurious light. *The New American Bible* says, in its commentary on Rahab, "*Harlot:*

this is the regular equivalent of the Hebrew word, but perhaps it is used here of Rahab in the broader sense of a woman who kept a public house. Joshua's spies hoped to remain undetected at such an inn." (NAB) Perhaps she did rent out rooms, but it does not make sense that this innkeeper was referred to as a harlot in her home town and continued to bear the derogatory title down through the centuries into the books of Hebrews and James. Is a woman a harlot simply because she is a business owner? Why is this commentary attempting to clean up her image?

Rahab is listed with Abraham in James 2:25. The text says, "And in the same way [as Abraham] was not also Rahab the harlot justified by works when she received the messengers and sent them out another way?" (RSV) The commentary in *The Oxford Annotated Bible* says, "Abraham and Rahab represent two extremes: the friend of God and the harlot; but both were justified by God." (RSV) The text does not say they represent two extremes. It says that the justification of Rahab and Abraham was the same. Jesus is reported to have spent time in the company of prostitutes. Is it not possible to be both a prostitute and a friend of God? This interpretation does not attempt to clean up Rahab's image but to discredit her importance and keep her firmly in the role of a less respected person.

Sometimes biblical women are just left out of biblical readings and commentaries. The daily reading for the Catholic Community on Friday, May 16, 2009 was James 2:14–24 and 26. The 25th verse of chapter two was left out. It is the chapter that specifically speaks of Rahab. We believe what we believe about Rahab because the commentators have either tried to leave her out, clean her up or discredit her.

Women were the property of their fathers until they were married. After they were married, they were the property of their husbands. But, Rahab turns this custom on end. She is the property owner; she is the one who negotiates a deal with the messengers to protect her family. Rahab is mentioned three times in the Christian Scriptures: first, in Matthew's genealogy of Jesus, second, in a list of the champions of faith found in Hebrews 11:31, and finally in James 2:25. Rahab, whoever this brave, resourceful woman was, deserves her place among the champions of faith, not cleaned up, discredited or ignored.

Where to Find Ruth's Story

The book of Ruth is one of only two books named for a woman in the Protestant Bible and one of only three books named for a woman in the Catholic Bible. The others are Esther in both the Catholic and Protestant Bibles and Judith in the Catholic Bible. The story of Ruth is found in the book named for her. Ruth does have a voice in her story. Unfortunately, she does not speak in the fourth and final chapter, nor does she name her own son.

Ruth Tells Her Story

> "I am Ruth. Spread your cloak over me. You are next of kin." (Ruth's request to Boaz when he wakes to find her sleeping at his feet on the threshing room floor in Ruth 3:9)

My name is Ruth. I am known as "The Moabite." I married into a Hebrew family living in Moab. My mother-in-law is very dear to me. She was a widow when I married her son. I lived with my husband for ten years but both my husband and my brother-in-law died. My mother-in-law, Naomi, my sister-in-law, Orpah, and I were devastated. Three widowed women have very few resources available to them. Naomi decided she would be better off if she returned to Judea, where she had family and property in a town called Bethlehem. She encouraged Orpah and me to go back to our mothers. We cried a lot during that time. We lost our husbands and now we were losing our dear mother-in-law.

Orpah finally decided to stay in Moab. I could not imagine what would happen to Naomi or to me if she left by herself so I made the decision to go with her. It was a very difficult, emotional and painful decision. When we got to her country, we had each other, a parcel of land and not much else. My mother-in-law was very depressed. She blamed her God for the death of her husband and her sons. When her old friends and family would meet her and ask, "Naomi, is that you?" she would answer, "Do not call me Naomi. That name means 'pleasant.' Call me Mara. That name means 'bitter.'"

It was the time of the harvest when we settled in Bethlehem. My mother-in-law and I needed to eat. Naomi had a relative named Boaz who was a wealthy landowner and a very kind, generous man. I knew the law allowed the poor to pick grain out of the fields after the reapers had passed. I asked the reapers' permission to gather grain. It was very hard work. Boaz came into the field as I was working and asked about me. He spoke to me kindly and told me to stay close to his workers and to the women in the field. He also told the workers not to molest me. The women who were working told me not to go into other fields because women got assaulted and sometimes raped. At lunchtime Boaz offered me food and told me I could drink the water the men had brought. It is usually women who bring water to the men. I was afraid the men would be angry with me for drinking their water, but Boaz spoke to them on my behalf. He even invited me to dip my bread into his wine. I was not a family member, but a woman and a foreigner. I was not sure what to make of his unusual kindness.

At the end of the day, I had a great deal of grain and some of my lunch left over so I had food for my mother-in-law. She was very surprised by how much grain and food I had. I told her I had been working in the fields of Boaz. She was glad he told me to stay in his field. There was, indeed, a great danger of being molested in other fields. My mother-in-law's depression was beginning to lift. I knew something was on her mind. I worked hard in the fields every day. Finally my mother-in-law told me what she had been planning. She knew that Boaz would be alone on the threshing floor that evening. She told me to bathe, put on perfume and my best dress and go to the threshing floor. I did as she instructed. I stayed in hiding until Boaz fell asleep after plenty of food and wine. I went to Boaz and lay beside him.

When he woke up, he was astonished that I was there. I was very bold and asked Boaz to marry me. He told me how much he cared for me and what a wonderful woman he thought I was. I spent the night with him on the threshing floor. Before it was light, Boaz gave me some more grain and sent me home. He watched as I left. I know he was trying to protect me.

When I got home, I told Naomi everything. She was very happy but told me to be patient. She had another relative and Boaz had to speak to him before he could marry me. The relative was willing to take the land that was Naomi's but did not want me.

Boaz and I were married. The elders wished for us blessings of abundance, with children to build up the house of Israel like Leah, Rachel and Tamar. I was overjoyed when I discovered I was pregnant. My child was a son.

When my son was born, there was great rejoicing. You would have thought it was my mother-in-law who had given birth. Her friends came to my home and praised God that Naomi had not been left without someone to carry on her family. Naomi embraced my son as if he were her own. Although the women of the village acknowledged me as the mother of my child and praised me for the value I had been to my mother-in-law, they did not embrace me as one of them. I was still Ruth the Moabite. They decided what they were going to call my son and referred to him as Naomi's next of kin. Naomi and I were secure, and, for that, I was grateful, but my heart was sad that I was not welcomed as a full member of the community.

Observations on Ruth's Story

The Book of Ruth is a biblical Cinderella story of sorts. Two poor, destitute women become celebrated members of their community in

Bethlehem because of the clever management of their circumstances by Ruth's mother-in-law, Naomi.

Ruth was a Moabite, the widow of a man from the tribe of Judah and the great-grandmother of King David. Moabites, according to Genesis 19:37, were descended from Lot's sexual union with his oldest daughter. Ruth was considered a foreign woman as were Tamar and Rahab, the Canaanites. Because of the fear of pollution by other religions, later biblical writers encouraged Israelite men to divorce their Moabite wives as well as other nationalities of women and disown the children from those unions. The law in Deuteronomy 23:4 states, "No Ammonite or Moabite shall be admitted to the assembly of the Lord." (NRSV) Ezra 10:3 declares, "So now let us make a covenant with our God to send away all these wives and their children, according to the counsel of my lord and of those who tremble at the commandment of our God." (NRSV) One can only imagine the heartbreak and hardship this caused the women, their children and perhaps the men who were sending them away!

Ruth is praised for her devotion to her mother-in-law Naomi. She leaves Moab and any family she had there to go to Bethlehem with Naomi. Ruth and Naomi would have had to travel around or over the Dead Sea to get to Bethlehem. In Bethlehem Ruth meets Boaz, a relative of Naomi. She gleans in his field to feed her mother-in-law and herself. When the harvest is over, Naomi encourages Ruth to wash, dress and go to the threshing floor where Boaz will be working that night. She further instructs her to hide until Boaz has finished eating and drinking and is lying down. Then she tells Ruth to uncover the feet of Boaz and lie down. "In Hebrew, *feet* can be a euphemism for genitals, thus giving a sexual overtone to Naomi's instructions and Ruth's subsequent actions." (NRSV)

When Ruth returns home the next morning, she tells her mother-in-law of her encounter with Boaz. This conversation is the last time we hear the voice of Ruth. She is silent for the rest of the story. She never tells us how she feels when the women of the town, not she herself, name her baby Obed. She never tells us about her marriage or of her great joy at the change of fortune in her family.

In Ruth's telling of her story, she says that she boldly asks Boaz to marry her. Ezekiel 16:8 says, "Again I passed by you and saw that you were now old enough for love. So I spread the corner of my cloak over you to cover your nakedness." (NAB) The commentary on that verse says, "I spread the corner of my cloak over you to cover your nakedness: and also to signify the intention of marriage." (NAB) The word "skirt," in the King James, can also be translated "cloak." Thus, when Ruth asks Boaz to spread his cloak or skirt over her, she is asking him to marry her. Ruth appears to be fearless and decisive. She leaves her home and family to travel with her mother-in-law. She risks molestation or worse in the fields to ensure that she and Naomi do not starve. She also secures a place in the community for herself and Naomi through her relations with Boaz.

The laws allowing the poor, the foreigner, the orphan and the widow to glean in the fields after the harvest are found in Leviticus 19:9–10; 23:22 and Deuteronomy 24:19. The language of social justice describes this as God's special option for the poor. The poor, foreign, orphaned and widowed would have been the powerless members of society. Ruth is a poor widow and a foreigner. She is a triply marginalized woman, powerless and without authority.

The story of Ruth is the story of two women who change their fortunes by the use of the few resources available to them. If "feet" is used here as a euphemism for "genitals," then Ruth, with the encouragement of Naomi, has used her sexuality to transform her circumstances. At the very least, she has placed Boaz and herself in a compromising situation. She is said to rise so early that no one would recognize her, and Boaz declares that he does not want anyone to know that a woman has been there that night. Additionally, Boaz calls her "Blessed of the Lord" when he wakes up to find her sleeping with him. She is further praised for her virtue because she has not gone after young men. It was because of her unorthodox actions that she became the great-grandmother of King David.

It appears that the narrator of this story uses the actions of the women in the village to erase the Moabite, the foreign woman. The women of the village name the child and say that a son has been born to Naomi. Ruth does not tell us how she feels about this turn of events. And yet this foreign woman and her unconventional actions further the line of David and the genealogy of Jesus.

Where to Find Bathsheba's Story

More than any woman in the Bible, with the exceptions of Eve and Mary Magdalene, the interpretations of Bathsheba's story have distorted our view of this woman and the circumstances of her life. She was not the temptress she has been portrayed to be. She was a woman caught in the schemes of a powerful man. Her story appears in Second Samuel 11:1–27; 12:1–25 and First Kings 1:1–2:25. She is also mentioned in the introduction to Psalms 51 and First Chronicles 3:5.

Bathsheba Tells Her Story

"I am pregnant!" (Bathsheba to David in Second Samuel 11:5)

I am an old woman now. I am the queen mother. When I was a young wife, I never imagined that my life would turn out as it has. I was married to Uriah. He was the armor bearer for Joab, the general of the king. My husband was a very honest, righteous man. We loved each other very much. He would call me his little lamb. When he was home I would sleep with my head on his chest.

Our home was a short distance from the palace of the king. It was a small two-story house built around a courtyard. Like our neighbors, we kept our animals on the ground floor. We set up tents on our roof when the weather was nice. From there we could do our household tasks in the fresh air. Sometimes it was not very pleasant to be inside with all the animals in the house.

One afternoon I was performing the ritual cleansing required by law for all women after their period. I had no idea that the ritual bath I was performing would change my life and that of Uriah's forever.

Later that evening some men came to my home and took me to the palace. The king had been spying on me while I bathed. He demanded that I have sexual relations with him. I hated him for the power he had over me. When he was finished, he sent me back to my home.

I was hoping to just put the whole experience out of my mind. What could I do? The penalty for intercourse with a man who was not my husband was stoning. It would break Uriah's heart to have me stoned, but he was a righteous man who kept the law.

I was devastated when the time for my period came and went and I did not have my period. My worst fears had been realized. I sent word to the king that I was pregnant. He had to know that the child was his. My husband was away on a campaign, and the king knew that the bath I was taking when he was spying on me was my ritual cleansing. To my great surprise, I heard the king had sent for my husband.

I have never been quite clear about what happened next. The king would never talk about it. What I have been able to glean is this. The king sat down with my husband and questioned him about how the war was going. Then he suggested that Uriah come home to me for the evening. Uriah would never do that. He had been consecrated for war. Instead he slept where the other members of the army slept.

When the king found out that Uriah had not come home, he questioned him again. Rumor had it that he tried to get Uriah drunk but being the righteous man he was, Uriah still did not come home. If he had, he might be alive today.

I heard the king sent a note to the general ordering him to put Uriah in the front of the battle, where the fighting was the fiercest and to pull the other troops back, leaving Uriah to be killed. I have never been told for sure that the king was responsible for his death, but I suspect the rumors were true. I do know my husband was such an honorable man that if the king sent his death warrant with him, Uriah would not have read it unless instructed to do so.

My husband was killed, and I was heartbroken. If the rumors about the king's actions were true, I was furious and terrified. I was pregnant, my husband was dead, and the child I was carrying was not my husband's. If anyone cared to figure out how long he had been at war and how long I had been pregnant, I was in big trouble. What would happen to me now?

I mourned the loss of my husband and the life we had planned together. When my time of mourning was over, the king sent messengers to my home a second time. They took me to the palace. It was there that I met the prophet Nathan. We became friends, and I told him how I had come to be living in the palace. He interceded for me. He confided to me that he told the king a parable about a rich man and a poor man. The parable was really about Uriah and me. In the parable, the poor man had nothing, except one little ewe lamb. The poor man nourished the lamb, which grew up with him and his children. She shared what little food the man had, drank from his cup and slept on his bosom. She was like a daughter to him. The rich man slaughtered the poor man's lamb to make a meal for his guests. Nathan told me the king became very angry with the actions of the rich man in the story. The king said the rich man should die and restore the poor man's lamb fourfold. Nathan told the king that what he had done to me and to Uriah was worse than what the rich man had done to the poor man. The king realized how wrong he had been. My heart was broken, like the heart of the poor man in the story! To this day, I am called the wife of Uriah.

The king behaved very strangely after my baby was born. He prayed and wept for my baby as it struggled to live. He fasted, and slept on the ground clothed in sackcloth. My baby lived for only seven days. Nathan said it was the king's punishment for what he had done to

Uriah and me. Why did my baby have to die to punish the king? I felt like I was the one being punished, and I had done nothing wrong! My heart was broken a second time.

As soon as the king found out my baby was dead, he got up, washed himself and requested food. When his servants asked him why he was behaving so strangely now that the baby was dead, he answered, "As long as the child was alive, there was a chance that God might grant that it continue to live. Now that it is dead, why should I fast? It won't bring him back."

The king did his best to comfort me. I eventually had four more sons. My son Solomon became king but not without a lot of work on my part. I always had to have my wits about me. The king had many wives and concubines, consequently many children and many problems.

The prophet Nathan was always my biggest ally. He found out that the king's son Adonijah had declared himself king. Adonijah had prepared a feast and invited, among others, the priest Abiathar, who was calling Adonijah king. Nathan knew that if Adonijah became king, Solomon and I would be killed. We devised a plan and conspired with the king to have Solomon ride the king's mule to Gihon and there to have Solomon anointed king by the priest Zadok and Nathan the prophet.

My son is a good and wise king. He is respectful to me, listens to me, and has a throne for me beside his own. I have had a good life, but some days I wonder what my life with Uriah would have been if he had not been killed.

Observations on Bathsheba's Story

On Friday June 26, 2009, South Carolina governor Mark Sanford apologized to his cabinet for his extramarital affair. The reporter from *Good Morning America,* John Hendren, who reported on the governor's apology, introduced the governor by saying, ". . . comparing himself to the biblical king who gave in to the temptress Bathsheba . . ." This attitude, or perhaps lack of knowledge, demonstrates the necessity for writing these women's stories. Bathsheba is maligned as a temptress. The biblical text does not say that Bathsheba was a temptress, nor does it imply in her actions that she was a temptress. Unfortunately, this misconception about Bathsheba is the one that pervades our culture.

The scriptural evidence that King David was a voyeur is effectively ignored. He is told Bathsheba's father is Eliam. Perhaps he is the same Eliam who is listed with Bathsheba's husband, in Second Samuel 24:34, with David's thirty-seven elite. He knows her husband and father. This is of no importance to David. What David does when Bathsheba is brought to him sounds more like rape than the beginning of a love story. Had she not become pregnant, the story might have ended there. In fact, the king wanted the story to end there, which is why he sent for Uriah and tried to get him to go home on two different occasions to sleep with his wife. The implication is that the king will be able to pass off his child as Uriah's. Uriah, being an honorable man, does not go home but sleeps amongst the troops. "Continence was required of soldiers consecrated for war by religious sanction. Uriah refused to violate this taboo even when David made him drunk." (RSV) When David realizes that he will not be able to pass the child off as Uriah's, David arranges to have Uriah killed.

Bathsheba's story begins in Second Samuel 11:1. The title given for this section in *The New American Bible* is "David's Sin." The *Oxford Annotated Bible* describes it as "David Wrongs Uriah." This is certainly true. David did sin, and Uriah was wronged, but so was Bathsheba! She was a powerless woman put into a compromising position by a powerful man. "During Uriah's absence in the wars, David forced her to commit adultery with him. Uriah was then treacherously killed by David's order."[2]

---

[2] J. D. Douglas and Merrill C. Tenney, ed., *The New International Dictionary of the Bible* (Grand Rapids: Zondervan Publishing House, 1987), 129.

After the period of mourning for Uriah had passed, the king had Bathsheba brought to his palace. Bathsheba mourned the death of her beloved husband. The clues to the relationship between Uriah and Bathsheba are in the condemnation of the king by the prophet Nathan. Nathan compares Uriah and Bathsheba to a poor man who has nothing but one little ewe lamb that grew up with his children, ate his meager food, drank from his cup and lay in his bosom. Nathan describes a very loving relationship between Uriah and Bathsheba. The prophet continues to be an advocate for Bathsheba and her son, Solomon, throughout her life. If she was a temptress and seduced the king, it does not seem likely that the prophet of God would advocate for her.

God is said to be very angry with David. Bathsheba's child dies as God's punishment of the king, and Bathsheba is forever branded a temptress. Why has a story of voyeurism, murder, and seduction (if we are to give the king the benefit of the doubt and not call what he did rape) been turned into Bathsheba as temptress? The answer is simple. Blame is placed squarely on the victim. "Historically, society has viewed sexual violence against women as the victim's problem. Rape was a dark secret not openly discussed. The woman was pathologized. Something within her caused the incident. She was a victim of her own actions and choices."[3] David, the king and biblical hero, of whom it is said in Acts 13:22 is "a man after God's own heart," is off the hook. Why do we believe what we do about Bathsheba? Because it is easier to believe that the woman was at fault than to hold the male biblical hero accountable for his actions. It is time to hold David accountable for his actions and stop branding Bathsheba as a temptress.

---

[3] Alida V. Merlo and Jocelyn M. Pollock, eds., *Women, Law, and Social Control 2 ed.* (Boston: Pearson Education Inc., 2006), 150.

Conclusion

Rahab, Ruth and Bathsheba were three unconventional foremothers of Jesus. None of them started their lives as members of the tribe of Israel. Rahab was a Canaanite. If her story were written by the Canaanites of the city of Jericho, she would be remembered as a traitor to her people and not as a champion of faith. Ruth the Moabite, like Sarah, leaves her homeland. Like Tamar, her unconventional actions ensure her survival and the continuation of the genealogy leading to King David. Finally, Bathsheba, who, like so many women, survives cruel circumstances to make the best life she can for herself and her children.

Chapter Four

WOMEN IN JESUS' FAMILY

Light University, a Ministry of the American Association of Christian Counselors Foundation, offers a certificate program in biblical counseling and women's ministry. Tim Clinton, the president of Light University, is also a professor at Liberty University. Liberty University, like the Roman Catholic Church, does not believe God calls women to the ordained ministry despite evidence found in Scripture that women were indeed prophets, preachers and teachers. It was the woman known as "the woman at the well" who first evangelized her village and converted many with the good news of the Messiah. It is women who were the first commissioned to preach the good news of the risen Christ. The description of course EW103, offered by Light University, A Woman's Soul: Self-Concept, Identity & Fulfillment, uses these words to describe the class: "Finding fulfillment in life is dependent on a woman knowing who she is in Christ." If this is true, it is essential that we understand Jesus and his relationships with the women in his life and his culture. Because Jesus' relationship with the male disciples has been stressed in the stories about Jesus, we sometimes forget the many women in Jesus' life.

The stories of the women have not been recorded in detail. It is the stories of the men that are recorded. Women appear in "supporting" roles. Who were the women? What was the relationship between Jesus and these women? How do we believe Jesus treated women? Jesus is reported to have broken cultural and religious barriers in his interactions with lepers, tax collectors, the ritually unclean and other members of society who religious leaders did not consider valuable. Did Jesus break cultural and religious barriers in his associations with women as well, or did Jesus reinforce the injustices of his time? If we believe Jesus is God incarnate, would Jesus reinforce *any* injustice? I believe Jesus modeled a wonderful and radical new way of being in relationship with one another. I also believe the evidence in Scripture of Jesus' equal treatment of women.

It is important to remember that none of the gospel writers knew Jesus or were eyewitnesses to the events recorded in the gospels. For many years the stories of Jesus were passed on orally. The gospel attributed to Mark is believed to be the first written biblical gospel. "Traditionally, the gospel is said to have been written shortly before A.D. 70, in Rome, at a time of impending persecution and when destruction loomed over Jerusalem." (NAB) That is approximately forty years after the life of Jesus. Scholars believe Matthew and Luke used information found in Mark and other written and oral sources in the composition of their gospels.

These gospels were not the only writings about the life of Jesus. Luke says in the introduction to his gospel, "Since many have undertaken to set down an orderly account of the events that have been fulfilled among us, just as they were handed on to us by those who from the beginning were eyewitnesses and servants of the word, I too decided, after investigating everything carefully from the very first, to write an orderly account for you, most excellent Theophilus, so that you may know the truth concerning the things about which you have been instructed." (NRSV) Matthew was written sometime after Mark and Luke, probably about 85 C.E. John, the latest of the biblical gospels, is dated between 90 and 100 C.E. "This is widely accepted by the vast majority of scholars across denominational lines, including across the 'liberal'/'conservative' divide."[1]

Who were the women in Jesus' family? Unlike most women in the Bible, Mary, the mother of Jesus, has a voice, although most of her story is told *about* her, rather than *by* her. We are given very few glimpses into the relationship between Jesus and his mother, even though she appears in all four gospels and in the *Acts of the Apostles.*

Many stories and legends have grown up around Mary, apart from what is recorded in the text. From Matthew and Luke, we get conception and birth stories about Mary and her son. Mark and John are silent on the subject. Jesus' sisters appear three times in the gospels. Unfortunately, their names have been lost to us, and their unique experience of having Jesus as their brother was not recorded. The Catholic Church, in its attempt to promulgate the medieval doctrine of Mary's perpetual virginity, negates the possibility of his having had siblings.

Jesus' aunt stands with her sister, Mary, at the foot of the cross. In John 19:25, she is called "his mother's sister." Finally, there is Elizabeth, the mother of John the Baptizer. She is called a "kinswoman" of Mary in Luke 1:36. I suspect she is Mary's aunt because she is described as "getting on in years" in Luke 1:7 and as "a relative in her old age" in Luke 1:36. The *Illustrated Dictionary and Concordance of the Bible* calls Mary the cousin of Elizabeth. It seems much more likely that Mary was her niece due to the references to Elizabeth's advanced age. Following are the imagined stories of the women in Jesus' family.

Where to Find the Story of Mary, the Mother of Jesus

Mary's story is found in only twelve places in the entire Bible. Matthew 1:18–25; 2:1–23; 12:46–50; 13:53–58; Mark 3:31–35; 6:1–6; Luke

1 Nancy Corran, written message to author, July 2011.

1:26–56; 2:1–52; 8:19–21; John 2:1–12; 19:25–27; and Acts 1:14.[2] Mary tells her story as it relates to her son. Her sister tells the story of Mary and her son. All we know of Mary's sister is that she was at the cross of Jesus with Mary. John 19:25 says, "Meanwhile, standing near the cross of Jesus were his mother and his mother's sister." (NRSV) Imagine, Jesus had an aunt, the sister of his magnificent mother! What must the aunt of Jesus have been like? We cannot know, but we can imagine what her relationship with her sister and her nephew might have been.

Visualize the spectacular woman Mary must have been. She gave birth to and raised the child, Jesus, a person, on whose life and teachings a new religion was founded. Luke's gospel calls her "the favored one of God." The travels of Mary and her family are different in Matthew and Luke. The "nativity" of Mary does not appear in Mark, the first Gospel written, nor in John, the last Gospel written. In Matthew's story, the family is in Bethlehem. They flee to Egypt and come back to settle in Nazareth. In Luke's story, the family is in Nazareth, goes to Bethlehem, travels to Jerusalem and then returns to Nazareth. In Matthew's story, Mary is visited by the Magi; in Luke's story, it is the shepherds who visit Mary. The two differing nativity narratives found in Matthew and Luke are harmonized in the account of the birth of Jesus told by the sister of Mary and in Mary's telling of her own story, much the way they are harmonized in Christmas celebrations.

Imagine if the voice of Mary's sister had been recorded!

My Sister's Story

> "How can I be pregnant? I am a virgin." (Mary cries to her sister, upon discovering that she is pregnant. Imaginative reconstruction of Luke 1:34)

---

[2] Miriam Therese Winter, *Woman Word: A Feminist Lectionary and Psalter—Women of the New Testament* (New York: Crossroad, 1994), 12.

My sister, Mary, is an extraordinary individual. Everyone has always thought so. When the women are alone together, they say they are sure Mary could have been a Rabbi if she had been born a boy. My sister is intelligent, poetic, spiritual, wise and introspective. Her firstborn son was much like her. Our father arranged a good marriage for my sister with a man named Joseph. While my sister was still living in our parents' home, she discovered she was pregnant. She was terrified, and so was I. Our law states that if a girl is not a virgin when she marries, she is to be brought to the entrance of her father's house and the townsmen are to stone her to death. I was the one in whom she confided. We tried to figure out a solution to this situation. She could take a bloody sheet to the elders at the city gate as evidence of her virginity. But as we all knew, she had not gone to the home of Joseph yet, so, of course, there was no evidence of her virginity. Even if she could produce the evidence, it was so humiliating for a woman to have to take a bloody sheet to the city gate so all the elders could look at it and proclaim that the woman was a virgin on her wedding night. We talked late into the night about how this had happened and what she should do. Mary insisted she had not had sexual relations with Joseph or anyone else. She told me things that did not make any sense to me. She told me she had a vision of an angel. The angel told her she was favored by God and that God was with her. The angel told her she would have a son. The more complicated the story became, the more I was afraid she had been drinking too much new wine.

While all this was happening, we found out that our Aunt Elizabeth was six months pregnant. What a blessing for her! We decided the best thing for Mary to do was to visit our aunt. She could leave under the pretense of going to help Elizabeth with the pregnancy and birth of Elizabeth's child. Elizabeth would need help. She was quite old to be having a child. I could not endure the thought of my remarkable sister being stoned to death on my parents' doorstep. Mary stayed with Elizabeth for three months until Elizabeth's son, John, was born.

After Mary left to visit Elizabeth, I had to tell Joseph about the pregnancy. As I said, he was a good man. Joseph understood the commandments and ordinances. He knew he was not the father of the child. He knew Mary would be stoned to death when the pregnancy was discovered. He decided to divorce my sister quietly, thinking perhaps that if the men of the town did not find out about the pregnancy, Mary would not be put to death. Joseph, however, had a change of heart. He was like my sister in many ways. He told me that he had seen an angel in a dream. The angel told him not to be afraid, that the child Mary was carrying was from the Holy Spirit. Both Joseph and my sister were convinced the child would be a boy.

Life was not easy for my sister. When it was almost her time to deliver, she and Joseph had to travel from Nazareth to Bethlehem for the census. It was not an easy journey in the best of circumstances, and my sister was nine months pregnant. The four-day journey took a week because they had to cross the Jordan River and go around Samaria to get to Bethlehem. When they finally got to Bethlehem, they could not find anywhere to stay. My sister gave birth to her son in a place where farm animals feed. My nephew's first bed was a trough.

I did not see my sister or my nephew for many years. When I did see her, she had some fantastic stories to tell!

According to Mary, thirty-three days after the birth of her son, she and Joseph took him to Jerusalem to the temple. Our law says that a woman who has given birth to a son is unclean for thirty-three days. The law requires that Mary take a lamb and a turtle dove for an offering. Mary and Joseph were poor. They could only afford two turtle doves. One of the doves was a purification offering; the other was a sin offering.

In the temple they met the prophet Anna. She prophesied to all who would listen about the future she envisioned for my nephew. Shortly after their trip to the temple, Mary and Joseph took Jesus and left Jerusalem to go to Egypt. Joseph had a dream in which God told him to flee because the king wanted to destroy my nephew. I was very unhappy that they were not returning home, but I remembered that it was a dream which had persuaded Joseph not to divorce my sister. That dream had probably saved her life. My nephew was three years old before any of his family got to meet him.

When my nephew was twelve years old, our extended family traveled to Jerusalem for the feast of the Passover. We were a very large group. It was not until we had traveled a full day's journey on our way home from Jerusalem that Mary realized her son was not with us. She thought he was traveling with some of our family members. We didn't know it at the time, but Jesus had stayed behind on purpose. Mary was frantic. She and Joseph returned to Jerusalem and searched for him for three days.

Finally, they found him in the temple. My sister is usually gentle and soft-spoken but not this time! "Son," she cried, "why have you done this to us? Your father and I have been looking for you frantically!" Mary told me my nephew tried to get out of the trouble he was in by saying he had waited in the temple, where he was safe until they came back for him. I do not know what else she said to her son, but Jesus came home and was a very obedient child from then on. Mary said when they found Jesus, he was doing something she had always wanted to do. He was sitting in the midst of the teachers, asking questions and listening to the answers. One of the teachers told Joseph that Jesus had understanding and wisdom beyond his years. I can remember the women saying the same thing about Mary when we were little. I know that my nephew learned so much from my precious sister. It was a joy to watch him increase in wisdom under my sweet sister's teaching.

When the end came for my nephew, it was more horrible than I could have ever imagined. I was with my sister at his cross. Her bravery was awe-inspiring. There were many women with us: beloved Mary Magdalene, Joanna, Mary the mother of James, Salome, Susanna and so many other women who had traveled with my nephew and ministered to him from their own possessions.

I was ashamed of the men who had called themselves his friends. The night my nephew was arrested, the men deserted him and ran away. Peter denied to a servant girl that he even knew him. It is no wonder Jesus called him "the rock." He sometimes behaved so badly and never seemed to get Jesus' message.

The night Jesus washed our feet, Peter said to him, "You will never wash my feet." Jesus told Peter if he did not understand the symbolism of the feet washing, he would have no share in the work. Jesus wanted us to know we were to serve each other. Washing the feet of a guest was the act of a servant. None of us were to be masters or lords over others. We were equals and must treat each other as equals. Once Jesus even called Peter Satan and told him to get behind him. When Jesus was arrested, the men went into hiding, afraid for their own skin. It was the women who continued to follow Jesus, even to his death, the way we had ministered to him in his life. We didn't give a thought to the danger we were putting ourselves in. Jesus needed to know he was not abandoned, and we wanted to be there for him.

Observations on the Story of Mary's Sister

Following a presentation I gave regarding my "discovery" of Mary's sister at the foot of the cross, a Catholic woman informed me that I was wrong, "Mary was an only child." I asked, "The Gospel writer was wrong?" "Oh my," she said, "I must go talk to my priest!" She scurried off.

The legend of St. Ann, the mother of Mary, is based on the Protoevangelium of James, written in the mid-second century, and does indeed claim Mary's status as an only child. It also claims that Mary was consecrated to God and raised in the temple, much as the virgin priestess of the Roman goddess Vesta. These women are referred to as Vestal Virgins. John, however, clearly states in 19:25, "Standing near the cross of Jesus were his mother and his mother's sister." (NRSV) Mary's sister is not named in the gospel of John or anywhere else. Mary is not named in the gospel of John. She is simply referred to as the mother of Jesus. If the Gospel of John were the only gospel to survive, we would not know the name of the mother of Jesus. We can only imagine the enormous gaps in our knowledge of Jesus, upon whom Christianity was founded.

It makes sense to me, based on my relationships with my sisters, that the first person Mary would tell about an unexpected pregnancy would be her sister. Given the consequences of an unwed pregnancy, the situation must have seemed very grim. Although we are not told anything about the relationship between Mary and her sister, the fact that she is reported to be at the cross of her nephew indicates that there was a loving, supportive relationship between them.

It does not make sense to me that Mary would go to visit Elizabeth for three months and leave just before the birth of Elizabeth's child, as Luke 1:56–57 seems to imply. Women know that women stand by each other in times of need.

Because of the importance of Jesus to the Christian faith, we read the story of Jesus as a child in the temple with an emphasis on Jesus' special knowledge, questions, answers and understanding of his relationship with God. We do not read the story with an emphasis on Mary's feelings and her reaction to Jesus' decision to stay behind in Jerusalem. Imagine your twelve-year-old child missing in a big city for five days. Mary and Joseph were a full day's journey from Jerusalem and had to retrace their steps. They looked for him for three days before they found him. How frantic Mary must have been! Imagine further, that when you find your child, you learn s/he stayed in the city on purpose and then gives you a smart answer. I paraphrase, "Why were you looking for me? Didn't you know I'd be here?" The story continues in Luke 2:51: "Then he went down with them and came to Nazareth, and was obedient to them." (NRSV) I bet he was! Jesus, in human terms, had been very naughty.

Unless the contemporary reader is familiar with the laws recorded in Leviticus and Deuteronomy, we miss concerns relevant to the life of Mary and her son in the nativity stories. In Matthew's version of Mary's story, we are told that Joseph was going to divorce her quietly, so as not to expose her to public disgrace. We are left with the impression that Joseph is a nice guy and Mary does not have a much bigger problem than an out-of-wedlock pregnancy. But Deuteronomy 22:20–21 decrees that a woman who marries and is not a virgin is to be stoned to death by the men of the town.

Jesus is said to be confronted with a similar situation in John 8:21. A woman who has been accused of adultery is brought to him. The men who have brought her are ready to stone her to death, but Jesus intervenes on her behalf and the murder is stopped. Did Jesus know his mother could have suffered a similar fate and he might never have been born?

In Luke 2:24, Mary and Joseph offer two pigeons as a sacrifice after the birth of Jesus. Leviticus 12 prescribes the laws incumbent on the mother after the birth of a child. There are two stages of impurity. The first stage during which she can pollute anything she touches is seven days if her child is a boy and fourteen days if her child is a girl. If the shepherds and the magi visited Mary on the night of the birth of her child, they would have encountered a ritually unclean woman. In the second stage, it is only the holy that she can pollute. This stage lasts thirty-three days if the child is a boy and sixty-six days if the child is a girl. For the woman to become "clean," she must present a lamb and a pigeon or dove to the priest for a sacrifice. If she is too poor to afford the lamb, she may offer two pigeons or two doves. For the purposes of purification, Mary offered this sacrifice. When Mary took her sacrifice to the temple, she would have been allowed no further into the temple than the court of the women. Similarly, when she finds her son in the temple, she would not have been allowed past the court of the women.

From our twenty-first-century perspective, the impurity of a woman after the birth of a child, boy or girl, is inexplicable. Jesus is portrayed as a champion for the members of his society whom the religious leaders viewed as unclean and impure. He was an advocate for lepers, prostitutes, tax collectors, children and, perhaps, women like his mother, who were ritually unclean for as long as sixty-six days. His care of the hemorrhaging woman certainly demonstrates his compassion for marginalized women.

Jesus is said to wash the feet of the disciples. This and other references to feet in the Christian Scriptures are not euphemisms for genitalia. Jesus, by taking off his robe and tying a towel around himself, demonstrates the humility required of a disciple.

Mary's sister must have had great insight into Mary and her son. If she was with them at the cross, she must have supported the movement in some way. Imagine what we could learn if Mary's sister had written about Mary and Jesus. Imagine if the gospel writers had recorded what Mary said and thought about her son and his purpose. Imagine if Mary had written what she, herself, experienced!

Mary Tells Her Story

> "Jesus, why have you done this? We have been looking frantically for you for days." (Mary's question to her son in Luke 2:48)

My first born son was born in Bethlehem. Everything surrounding his conception and birth had been otherworldly and overwhelming. It started with a vision I had of an angel. The angel told me I had found favor with my God and I was to conceive a son. I was frightened and mystified. My father had promised me to Joseph, but I had not yet gone to Joseph's bed. In my vision, I saw my son as a great leader. I even imagined his name: Jesus. It means "God has saved." I was truly stunned when I realized that I really was pregnant—stunned and terrified.

I went to my sister first. We had always been very close, and I could confide anything to her. We were desperate to find a solution to this situation. When we found out that our Aunt Elizabeth was pregnant, I decided to go visit her. I needed to get out of town before my pregnancy was discovered. I knew only too well what the law required if I was found to be pregnant before Joseph and I had consummated our marriage.

Elizabeth was overjoyed to see me. She had a special insight into my pregnancy that I cannot explain. She knew I had been blessed. I felt less frightened with Elizabeth. She seemed to understand what I was going through and was not judgmental of me. I stayed until Elizabeth had her baby.

When I returned home, I was afraid of what might happen to me. I was three months pregnant by then. To my surprise and delight, Joseph was glad to see me. He welcomed me into his home and welcomed my pregnancy as if he were the father. He was a very good man! He was not afraid to take me as his wife. Joseph, it seems, also had a vision. I was sure the vision was from God.

Around the time for me to deliver my child, Joseph and I had to travel to Bethlehem to be registered. That was a very difficult trip. When we got to Bethlehem, there was nowhere for us to stay. Luckily, Joseph found a shed where animals were kept. I had my child there without a midwife or any other woman to help me. I wrapped my son in strips of cloth to keep him warm and put him to sleep in the trough where the animals were fed.

Seven days later, the shepherds who kept their sheep in that shed showed up. They declared they had a vision about the birth of my child but waited seven days because of the potential of being polluted by an "unclean" woman. They spoke of their own vision of angels who told them to come and see the child born in the stables.

I was not surprised by the visit of the humble shepherds. It was, after all, their region. However, I was surprised by the visit of the astrologers from the East. They brought some very expensive gifts, gifts fit for a king. It was a good thing they did. Joseph had a dream that my son was in danger. After the departure of the astrologers, we prepared to flee to Egypt. The gifts helped finance our trip. Before we left, we presented Jesus at the temple, as our law requires. I made my sin offering and purification offerings. Then we fled to Egypt. My son grew wise and wonderful.

Observations on Mary's Story

Many legends have developed around the twelve appearances of Mary in the Bible. She is said to be both virgin and mother, a very difficult feat for most women. In 1854, Blessed Pius IX proclaimed the dogma of the Immaculate Conception of the Blessed Virgin and her exception from original sin. She is also said to be a perpetual virgin. The brothers and sisters of Jesus recorded in the Bible are thus near relatives, perhaps cousins or the children of Joseph, but not Mary. "In 1950, Pope Pius XII declared the dogma of the Assumption of Mary; that is, that Mary's body did not decompose in the grave but was reunited by God to her soul soon after she died."[3]

As many as are the legends and speculations about Mary, this must be said. Much is made of the broken and bleeding body of Jesus in his sacrificial act of bringing salvation into the world. But it is through the broken and bleeding body of Mary, in her act of giving birth to her son, that salvation first enters the world.

Mary, the Mother of Jesus, Tells the Story of Her Revolutionary Son

My son—my magnificent, wonderful son—was a wise child, wise beyond his years. My sister said he had an old soul. Where do I begin to tell you about this boy, grown into a man, who shared thirty years of my life? My son was an exceptional person. He was always challenging traditional beliefs. He was like no other person. He certainly became someone who was like no man I had ever met. I would like to think I was partly responsible for my son's unique ideas and perceptions of the world. He was very strong in his beliefs about right and wrong.

[3] *The New International Dictionary of the Bible* (1987), s.v. "Mary."

From a very early age, it was obvious that he had a deep concern for justice. He was particularly concerned with the people who were seen as inconsequential: women, children and the sick. There was so much injustice and cruelty all around us.

To understand my son, his words and actions, you must first understand the circumstances in which we lived. We were an occupied people. The Roman government and its soldiers kept us in order. Punishment for any disobedience was swift and brutal. Our rulers were Romans or the puppets Romans had placed in power. Even the priests in the temple were appointed by the Roman government. Many people were looking for a messiah who would restore political control of our land to the Judeans.

Our culture was a patriarchy. The hierarchy consisted of rich and powerful men at the top and poor men in close proximity to the bottom. Women and their children were at the bottom, but widows, the childless and the ritually unclean were on the lowest rung. If a husband did not want a child, especially a girl child, he would simply leave it outside to die. Women, their children, widows and the sick were the most vulnerable members of our society. The wives and children of the rich and powerful men had life easier than other women and children, but they were not considered citizens.

My son was deeply religious and did not understand why the religious leaders made life so hard for so many. When he was twelve years old, he stayed in the temple in Jerusalem when we traveled there for Passover. He understood the commandments of God, but he wanted to understand why the Pharisees, the Sadducees and the Scribes made following the commandments so difficult, especially when the men in those groups couldn't agree among themselves on how the law was to be followed. The legalism of the religious leaders was something he never believed in and did not practice. His outspoken denunciation of them is one of the things that got him into so much trouble. He called them hypocrites and blind guides. He taught us not to do what they required because they placed heavy burdens on the people, but they didn't lift a finger to carry those burdens themselves. To Jesus the commandments were simple: "Love God with all your heart, soul and mind, and love other people as you love yourself." My son believed we should love ourselves because God loves us. He believed in the just reign of God on earth, a realm in which all were equal and none was of higher rank or more authority than another.

Jesus spent a long time in Galilee with his cousin John, called the Baptist. He was eventually baptized by John. Like my son, John believed in a renewal of the covenant between the people and our God. The baptism was symbolic of a change of heart. John called for people to realize that they had abandoned the practice of God's justice. He challenged people to repent of their injustices, be honest and kind, and to treat everyone as equally valuable. John's message and baptism were not just for men. He taught and baptized women as well. Many people were being baptized by John. When my son returned, he was changed. He had gone into the wilderness after the baptism. The experience of John's message and baptism had a profound effect on him.

And so his work began. What my son had to say about the reign of God on earth was good news to all who heard it, except to those in power. They had a lot to lose as people began to hear my son's message and change the way they treated each other and the way they lived before God. He began to surround himself with women and men for whom his message resonated. Of course, the women loved hearing his message, which was as much for them as for the men. One of his best friends was dear Mary Magdalene. She had been so ill before my son's healing presence in her life. There was fiery Salome and her sons. They were convinced that Jesus would establish the new government. Mary, Martha and Lazarus of Bethany were such good friends to my son. It was unusual for a man to have such close women friends, but my son saw the magnificence of everyone. Mary would sit and listen to Jesus teach, just like the boys who were allowed to go to school sat with their teachers. Joanna, who was the wife of Herod's steward, accompanied my son. Chuza and Susanna, among others, traveled with him and financed the group. It was extraordinary for women to travel freely with men who were not their husbands. Jesus' message was very liberating for women. My sister and I traveled with the group from time to time.

Jesus taught us about his vision of the reign of God on earth. He taught us how those who would be part of that realm should envision it. Children held no social status in our culture. When children tried to approach Jesus, his male friends would try to send them away. But Jesus, in his compassionate way, would always welcome children. He would take them in his arms or sit them on his lap. Jesus never missed an opportunity to teach us his vision of faithfulness to God and to each other. He would say, "See these innocent, trusting children? Unless you are like these children, there is no place for you in God's realm."

My son used imagery that women and the poor, in particular, would understand. He wanted to validate the worth of each of us. He also wanted us to realize how our understanding of God's realm could change the world. For example, women make the bread; they know how much yeast to put in the flour to make it rise. So Jesus compared the reign of God to the yeast a woman puts in flour until it is well leavened. His teachings were so surprising! He turned everything upside down. Sometimes he would offer caution against the leaven of the religious leaders, and then he would compare the leaven a woman puts in bread to the realm of God. Poor people understood the value of a poor woman's lost coin. So he taught about a poor woman who finds her lost coin. He believed that each human being was a treasure whether the religious leaders saw our value or not.

My son believed that the realm of God was present now, not in the distant future. Jesus believed that the realm of God was dependent on how those of us who wanted to be part of that realm treated each other. He did not see our religious leaders treating the people as if we were of equal value. He was highly offended that the temple would take the last coins of a poor widow instead of supporting her from their great treasury.

His faith in the power of God was so strong that he was able to manifest that power as only prophets could. But he believed if each one of us had faith like his, we, too, could manifest the power of God. He often told us that the wonderful things he could do, we could do also, if we had faith. My son did not use his power for himself but rather for people who suffered. He never forced his help on anyone, but if someone needed help, he would try to help them.

When he was teaching in the synagogue in Capernaum, there was a man everyone said was crazy and possessed by a demon. With a word, my son restored the man to his right mind. After that, many people came to my son to be restored. The religious leaders got very angry with him. They had such strict rules concerning what we could and could not do, especially on the Sabbath. Even helping someone on the Sabbath offended them. This grieved my son greatly. In my son's vision, people were more important than rules and laws; people were more important than the Sabbath and "everyone was worthy of rest from illness, especially on the Sabbath."[4]

My son's teachings were new, innovative and authoritative, "rooted in the prophets, law and wisdom,"[5] not like what we heard from the religious leaders. Those religious leaders were not too happy with what my son had to say about them, and they did not like the large crowds of people who came to listen to him. They were also very unhappy with the help my son offered the sick. In our culture, illness is viewed as a consequence of sin—a punishment from God—and here was my son doing whatever he could to alleviate suffering. Illness causes a person to become ritually unclean, and anyone who comes into physical contact with that person is unclean. My son did not agree with

---

4 Nancy Corran, written message to the author, July 2011.

5 *Ibid.*

the laws that punish the sick. If he met a person who was leprous or had a hemorrhage, he would touch them and not recoil.

On one occasion, some men lowered a man who appeared to be paralyzed down to my son through a hole in the roof. My son, being moved by the desperation of these men, said to the paralyzed man, "Your sins are forgiven." The religious leaders believed that illness was a sign of God's displeasure with a person. They taught that illness and poverty were a result of sin. In my son's view, illness, discrimination and poverty are the exact opposite of what God wants for us. The religious leaders were so angry when Jesus said, "Your sins are forgiven." The words of my son had a profound effect on that man, and he got up and walked away. The religious leaders were enraged, and the people were amazed. The religious leaders were always incensed when my son did something they didn't understand.

My son believed that all humans are the beloved children of God. He had great sympathy for all the people who the religious leaders thought of as impure or unclean. He was not afraid to share meals with tax collectors or prostitutes and other so-called "sinners." In fact, one of his best friends, Levi, was a tax collector who was despised because he worked for the Romans. Jesus understood that each one of us had, at one time or another, not lived up to our status as beloved children of God.

When he was in the temple one day, some of the religious leaders threw a woman at his feet. They wanted to stone her to death because they said she was caught having sex with a man who was not her husband. If they were truly concerned with following the law, they should have brought the man also. They were trying to trick my son into saying something against the law. Instead, my compassionate son asked if there were a man among them who had never broken one of the laws. That person, he said, should be the first to throw a stone at her. The woman's life was saved. My son always put people above the law.

As my son's ideas grew in popularity, I began to worry about him. He was not afraid to attack any establishment or social structure he saw as unjust. He did not believe in the patriarchal family structure in which men are privileged and women and children are the property of the men. He taught his followers not to call anyone on earth "father."

On more than one occasion, he taught large crowds. I went with some of our family to see him. Someone in the crowd sent word to him that we were outside asking for him. He said the people who did the will of God were his family, not necessarily the blood relatives standing outside in the crowd. He spoke of family as mother, sisters and brothers, equals in the family of God. There was no father, no authority figure in my son's vision of family. We knew that his words were not an affront to us. My son and I had always been very close, and I understood his thinking better than anyone. My son was calling for a challenge to accepted ideals.

He talked openly to women in public and in private. The Samaritan woman he met at Jacob's well presented a particularly shocking experience for his male friends and for her as well. Men simply did not speak to women in public, and Jewish men did not speak to Samaritans at all. Jesus shared his vision with her, and she understood. She was the first person to proclaim my son and his vision to people who were not his followers. Many people in her village came to believe in my son's vision because of the teaching of this woman.

I grew more and more worried about him. I knew he was making enemies of people in positions of power. John had been killed by Herod for far less than what my son was saying. In addition, he associated with tax collectors, he allowed "unclean" women to touch him, and he ate in the homes of known lepers. In the end, his loving, inclusive vision could not protect him from the authorities. After our last Passover meal, he and the men left for a walk in the garden. The rulers of the temple sent armed men to arrest him. I was never to caress my son again.

In the morning, we got word that he had been arrested and was to be crucified. We managed to pull ourselves together enough to find him and follow him to the place of crucifixion. It was more horrible than I could have ever imagined. None of the men were there. They had deserted him and fled, afraid for their own skins. The women were there! My sister, Mary Magdalene, Mary the mother of James, Salome and many women who had traveled with us to Jerusalem were all there. We stayed with my boy until it was over. Thank God he died quickly; some crucified people have been known to suffer for days! Joseph of Arimathea asked for his body and laid it in his own tomb. He was not given a proper burial.

Mary Magdalene and her companions returned to the tomb after the Sabbath to anoint his body and bury him properly, but his body was not there! The women saw visions of angels and ran back to tell us. Mary Magdalene stayed in the garden. It was there that she saw my son. She recognized him in the way he said her name.

In our culture, women are not allowed to give evidence in a court of law. My son believed the word of a woman had just as much honor and power as the word of a man. He sent her to tell the rest of us that he was alive and that he would see us soon. I was so disappointed in those men. They had deserted him, denied him and now they didn't believe that he had commissioned a woman with his most important message. They just didn't understand the inclusive nature of my son's vision. The other women and I remained with the community. We had to carry on without the physical presence of my son.

Observations on Mary's Story and that of Her Son

Faith in Jesus demands we understand, as much as is possible, about who Jesus was, what he said and what he did. Why did the short life of this man influence western history as significantly as it has? Why do we believe what we believe about Jesus? Do we believe in a flesh and blood man, a man who was God incarnate, the risen Christ?

Although I grew up going to church, it wasn't until church camp in 1971 that Jesus became real to me. The camp curriculum that year was titled "Jesus the Man." I began to realize why Jesus was the center of the religion I practiced. He wasn't just a name in a song or a name at the end of a prayer; he was a human being with a vision of justice and peace. The picture that developed was of a dynamic human being who did everything within his power to change the injustices in the world around him. Jesus practiced his Jewish faith and taught about faith in God within the context of Judaism. I believe Jesus' intent was to lead a renewal movement in his religion, not to form a new religion. He believed his renewal movement would reflect the purpose of God for creation and human relationships.

In the prayer he is reported to have taught his followers, he says, "Your will be done on earth as it is in heaven." Does it make sense that in heaven, whatever that truly means, God's will would be slavery, poverty, racism, gender discrimination, sickness or exploitation of any kind? These were the institutions, attitudes and injustices which Jesus the Man worked to expose and eliminate. Jesus proposed a radical challenge to tradition. He saw how the religious leaders interpreted the law, not for the sake of the people, but "for their own sake and for the sake of the institutions which supported them."[6] He practiced a model of service and communicated a message of inclusion which he left for us to follow. Jesus was so committed to the renewal of his religion that he was true to his philosophy even to a painful, humiliating death!

What can we imagine about the bond between Jesus and his mother? In John 2:3, Jesus and his mother have a brief conversation. The wine has run out at a wedding that both Jesus and his mother are attending. Mary informs her son of the situation. He appears to address her very disrespectfully saying, "Woman, what concern is that to you and to me?" (NRSV) Jesus also addresses his mother

6 *Ibid.*

as "Woman" while she stands at the foot of his cross in John 19:26. The Gentile woman is praised for her faith in Matthew 15:28 and addressed respectfully as "woman." According to *The New American Bible for Catholics,* this is "a normal, polite form of address." (NAB) Likewise, *The Oxford Annotated Bible* says this is "a term of solemn and respectful address." (RSV) Jesus is polite and respectful to his mother. We are told that Jesus traveled with his mother in John 2:12, along with others, to the seacoast town of Capernaum.

Jesus was human, a first-century Judean man. He ate and drank with his friends. He ate and drank with people who the religious establishment considered undesirable or worse. He did not fast "except in the wilderness after baptism"[7] as did John the Baptist, John's disciples and the religious leaders. He also appears to have been a wine drinker. In the story of the wedding in Cana, found in John 2:1–12, Jesus is said to turn water into wine—not just any wine but a wine that was superior to what had been served previously. *The New American Bible* translates the steward's response to the wine as, "Everyone serves good wine first, and then, when people have drunk freely, an inferior one." (NAB) I have often heard it said that wine, in this case, means grape juice. *The New Oxford Annotated* quotes the steward as saying, "After the guests have become drunk" (NRSV) indicating that the guests were drinking more than grape juice. As much as the divinity of Jesus and the saintliness of his mother are emphasized, they were humans, at a party, drinking wine and having a good time.

What have we been taught about The Last Supper? First, in Matthew, Mark and Luke, the gospels known as the Synoptic Gospels, Jesus is crucified on the day after the Passover meal. In the Gospel of John, written between 90 and 120 C.E. (some sixty to ninety years after the fact), Jesus is crucified on the day of preparation for the Passover. The story above follows the pattern found in the Synoptic Gospels.

[7] Nancy Corran, written message to the author, July 2011.

I was taught that there were twelve male disciples and Jesus in attendance at the Passover meal. Mark 14:12–17 says Jesus sent two disciples into the city to find a man carrying a jug of water. Carrying water was a job a woman, not a man, would have performed. The room to which the man carrying the water takes the disciples is furnished and ready. It is there that the disciples prepare the Passover meal. It is to that room that Jesus and the twelve come to eat after the meal has been prepared. Mark 14:17 says, "And in the evening he cometh with the twelve." (KJV) Disciples other than the twelve were in the room preparing the meal. The disciples were more than twelve men. We are told that women traveled with Jesus and ministered to him. We are told that women and the Mother of Jesus were at the crucifixion. We are told in Luke 2:41–42 that every year the parents of Jesus went to Jerusalem for the Passover and that they went, as usual, when Jesus was twelve years old. It does not make sense that Jesus would travel with men and women, including his mother, and the women would *not* be included in the feast which represents the most important event in Jewish history. Women would have been the disciples who prepared the meal.

In all four gospels, a collection of other women keep the vigil at the crucifixion and death of Jesus. Although each gospel presents a slightly different version of the crucifixion, Mary at the cross, along with the rest of the followers of Jesus on Pentecost, attests to her continued presence in the life and work of her son.

Where to Find the Story of Elizabeth

We have already met Elizabeth in the story of Mary. She is recorded once in Luke 1:5–80. Due to her barrenness, Elizabeth would have been looked upon with reproach, the belief being that she was barren because she had sinned and that God had prevented her from conceiving. Elizabeth is quoted in verse 25 as saying that God has taken away her reproach. Mary, on the other hand, had sinned by the very fact that she was unwed and pregnant.

Elizabeth Tells Her Story

"My son is named John." (Elizabeth tells the neighbors who wanted to name her son Zechariah in Luke 1:59)

I am Elizabeth, a descendant of the priestly line of Aaron. I was called a barren woman; I prayed for many years for a child. In our culture it is always women who must bear the shame of infertility, not men. There are many well-known women in my tradition who were infertile. The matriarch, Sarah, her daughter-in-law Rebekah, Rachel the sister of Leah, the mother of the legendary judge Samson, and Hannah the mother of the prophet Samuel. God is able to use even those whom society scorns. Female infertility is a great source of humiliation for women. It is viewed as a sign of God's displeasure. I lived my life faultlessly according to the laws of our people, but still my infertility remained. When I was past hope of conceiving a child, because I was getting old and post-menopausal, I discovered that I was pregnant. I secluded myself for the first five months of the pregnancy. I knew, at my age, that I needed to be very careful not to miscarry. I spent my time in prayer and thanksgiving for the blessing that had been given to me.

In the sixth month of my pregnancy, my niece Mary came to stay with me. She was pregnant also. The irony of my shame at being old and infertile, contrasted with Mary's shame at being a virgin and pregnant, was not lost on either of us. I was overjoyed to see her. She is a very extraordinary young woman. Her connection with the divine inside her is like none I have ever experienced. Her pregnancy paralleled mine in so many ways. She stayed with me for the next three months, until the birth of my son. We spent much time in prayer and praise for the miracle that had been done for both of us.

When my son was delivered, I named him John. My husband had a vision when he was serving in the temple that we had a son named John. Our relatives did not want to respect my choice of "John" as the name for my son, but my husband wrote, "His name is John."

There was gossip throughout the hill country of Judea. Why did they name him John? None of their relatives are named John. Why has Zechariah been silent since his service in the temple? Did he really have a vision? How could such an old woman have a baby? What will this child become? As for me, I was grateful to God for all the blessings that had come to my family. My son grew strong and spirited.

Observations on the Story of Elizabeth

The story of Elizabeth's barrenness, old age and miraculous conception echoes the experiences of Sarah, Rebekah and Rachel. Elizabeth names two other barren women in her story. They are Hannah, the mother of the prophet Samuel and Samson's mother. The name of Samson's mother has not been recorded. The Magnificat, the hymn which Mary sings in response to Elizabeth's exclamation in Luke 1:46–55, is reminiscent of the hymn of Hannah found in 1 Samuel 2:1–10.

The son to whom Elizabeth gives birth grows up to be John the Baptist, who prepares the way for Jesus. If, as I suspect, Elizabeth was the aunt of Mary, then John and Jesus are cousins. Zechariah, the husband of Elizabeth, is given instructions that the son to be born to Elizabeth is to drink no alcohol. Samson's mother, a woman like Elizabeth, who prayed to God for a child, is given a similar admonishment except it is Samson's mother who is to abstain from alcohol. Numbers 6:1–21 describes the vow of a Nazirite. The vow of the Nazirite is a temporary vow of holiness which both women and men can take. Among other requirements is the abstinence from alcohol. "Some of the restrictions accompanying the vow are similar to those for priests. Hence, a Nazirite enters a state of holiness similar to that of priests, albeit for a circumscribed time period." (NRSV) John the Baptist and the mother of Samson have taken the vow of the Nazirite. Both enter a state of holiness similar to that of a priest.

There is irony in the circumstances of Elizabeth, Mary and two of the women in Jesus' genealogy, Sarah and Tamar. Elizabeth and Sarah were old, married and past the age of child bearing. Mary and

Tamar were young, unmarried and pregnant. "The joining of these women's stories, whose central theme is the salvation and liberation of all people, occurs through the deliberate intervention of God, who weaves a storyline through women's wombs against all human odds."[8]

The Sisters of Jesus Do Not Tell Their Story

They may be found in Mark 3:31–35; 6:1–6, Matthew 12:46–50 and 13:53–58.

How many sisters did Jesus have? What were their names? What were their ages? What did they think of their brother Jesus? There is no story to go with the sisters of Jesus. They have no voice. They have no names. The brothers are named, but the sisters are not. They tell no story, and no story is told about them. Nothing is known about the sisters of Jesus except that they are said to be in Nazareth with their mother and brothers trying to see and speak to Jesus. These sisters of Jesus are further marginalized in the middle of the first century when the Catholic Church began to develop the doctrine of the perpetual virginity of Mary. The sisters are then said to be cousins or half-sisters, the children of Joseph but not of Mary and thus are denied a relationship even with their mother.

[8] This is not an exact quote. It is an adaptation of the words of Miriam Therese Winter.

Chapter Five

The Women Disciples of Jesus

There are women in all four Gospels who are reported to have accompanied Jesus and to have ministered to him. Joanna, Susanna, Salome the mother of the sons of Zebedee, and Mary the mother of James and Joseph. Mary Magdalene is the most well-known of Jesus' women friends. The sisters Mary and Martha of Bethany are also well-known friends of Jesus. The gospel of John in 1:5 says Jesus loved Martha and Mary. Perhaps, Mary, the wife of Clopas, was a friend of Jesus. John places her at the foot of the cross. She may also be one of the disciples on the road to Emmaus who is said to be traveling with Cleopas in Luke 24:18. Peter's mother-in-law may have become a friend of Jesus after he healed her. Peter's wife might also have been a friend of Jesus. She may have been angry with her husband because he quit his job and left her to follow an itinerant teacher, and angry with Jesus because he encouraged Peter to do so. Her name is never mentioned. However, in First Corinthians 9:5, Paul declares that Kephas (Peter), the other apostles, and Jesus' brothers travel with their wives. Among the friends and family of Jesus are the women who are in the upper room on Pentecost. The women, along with the men, were filled with the Holy Spirit.

Many legends have sprouted up around Mary Magdalene. Representations of her appear across the centuries in art and literature. The *Gospel of Mary* was discovered in 1896. It was likely written sometime between 120 and 180 C.E. To put this ancient date into perspective, the Gospel of John is dated between 90 and 120 C.E. Mary Magdalene is said to have traveled through the Mediterranean, preaching in the same manner as Peter and Paul. And, like Peter, she is said to have been martyred. Recently, she has been the subject of the action adventure novel and movie, *The Da Vinci Code.*

Where to Find Mary Magdalene's Story

Mary Magdalene is named in all four gospels. She must have played a significant role in the life of Jesus and the early church for her to be named so often, especially for a woman. Her story may be found in Mark 15:40–41, 47; 16:1–11; Matthew 27:55–56, 61; 28:1–10; Luke 8:1–3; 23:49, 55–56; 24:1–11; John 19:25; 20:1–18.

Mary Magdalene Tells Her Story

"Rabbi." (Mary's response to Jesus when he spoke her name in the garden in John 20:16)

I have been called the "apostle to the apostles." I was with Jesus throughout his travels and during his teaching. The other women and I provided money for the cause. It is a cause I believe in strongly. Meeting Jesus was the most healing experience of my life. I felt as if I had been liberated from the demons of our patriarchal society. Jesus treated women differently than other men treated us, even better than his male friends. Jesus treated all people as equals. Women, tax collectors, prostitutes, even lepers were treated as equals by Jesus. It is a life-changing experience to be accepted and respected by another person the way Jesus accepted and respected those who followed him and his teachings. I do not know a single person who was touched by Jesus and did not feel transformed.

Jesus did not believe in a hierarchy in our community. I will never forget the day the men were trying to decide who was greatest in the reign of God. Jesus set a child in front of them and told them that the humble child was greatest in God's realm and that they must become like that child. The social status of a child is not much better than that of a slave or a woman. This dispute continued right to the end of Jesus' life, although we did not know at the time that it was the end. Jesus set an example of service to others. He was our teacher, but we were equals. He told us, "I have given you a model to follow. Whoever would be the greatest among you must humble themselves and serve others." It was the way he treated everyone.

Jesus taught us in parables. Some of his parables used images of women to describe the reign of God. Images like maidens waiting for a bridegroom or a woman leavening her flour. My favorite was Jesus' image of God as a poor woman who has lost a coin. He described how she would sweep her house looking for the coin and when she found it would rejoice with her friends. Imagine, God with a broom performing the duties of a woman! Jesus' teachings were so innovative! How much more good could he have done if he hadn't been killed?

I was there for the whole dreadful event. Jesus and the men left after our Passover meal while we women stayed in the upper room. When the men returned, Jesus, Peter and Judas were not with them. The story they told of Judas' betrayal was unbelievable! I could only imagine how much Judas must be suffering. Peter had followed Jesus, but he did Jesus no good.

In the morning, we learned the horrible truth. Jesus, our revolutionary teacher, was to be killed. He was charged with political treason. The women and I went to the building where Jesus was being held. We followed Jesus on his way to the place of the skull outside the city wall. Years later, John would claim he was there, but none of us saw him. Jesus was always concerned for his disciples. He turned to us and called us "daughters" and warned us that this could be our fate also. We were not thinking of the danger we had put ourselves in by following a condemned political prisoner. He was our dear friend and teacher. We wanted to be there so he would know he was loved and not forgotten or abandoned. We waited with him until he died. Joseph of Arimathea took Jesus' body and laid it in his own tomb. We watched to see where Jesus' body was taken and went home to prepare spices for a proper burial.

When we returned after the Sabbath with the spices, his body was not there! What happened next is the reason I am called the "apostle to the apostles." I was the first person commissioned by the risen Christ to preach the good news of the resurrection. I was chosen to inform the disciples of what had transpired and instruct them as to how to proceed. Jesus entrusted this most important message to me, a woman. I remember that morning so well. I was distraught that the body of Jesus was gone. There was a man in the garden who I thought was the gardener. He asked me why I was crying. I begged him to tell me where the body of Jesus had been taken. And then he said my name. It was with such loving kindness that Jesus had always said my name. I recognized him in the way he said, "Mary." I threw my arms around him, my joy boundless! So gently he asked me not to hold on to him. That is when he commissioned me to proclaim the good news of his resurrection. As I was on my way to tell the men about our teacher, I remembered something he had said the last night we were together: Whoever receives the one I send receives me and whoever receives me receives the one who sent me. I was the one sent.

Observations on Mary Magdalene

Each gospel has a slightly different version of what happened at the crucifixion, burial and resurrection of Jesus. Matthew and Mark say there were bystanders and many women who had followed Jesus from Galilee and provided for him or ministered to him. In the Christian Scriptures, it is only women and angels who minister to Jesus. Matthew 27:55–56 names specific women: Mary Magdalene, Mary, the mother of James and Joseph and the mother of the sons of Zebedee. The list of the women in Mark 15: 40–41 is slightly different: Mary Magdalene, Mary, the mother of James the younger and Josses, and Salome. Luke 23:49 says all his acquaintances, including the women, stood at a distance. John 19:25–26 places Jesus' mother, her sister, Mary the wife of Clopas, Mary Magdalene, and the disciple whom Jesus loved at the foot of the cross. The disciple whom Jesus loved is presumed to be the narrator of the Gospel of John. The Gospel of John is the only Gospel which places John at the foot of the cross, hence the reference to John being the only one who thinks he was there. The constant is Mary Magdalene. Joseph of Arimathea is also a constant and is called a "disciple of Jesus." So we know that there were more than twelve who were considered disciples of Jesus. It is from the group of disciples that Jesus chooses the twelve in Luke 6:13.

The gospels also differ in their accounts of who goes to the tomb to anoint Jesus' body. Matthew tells us in 28:1 it is Mary Magdalene and "the other Mary" who go to the tomb. They are both commissioned by an angel and by Jesus to go tell the good news of the resurrection. In Mark's gospel, Mary Magdalene, Mary the mother of James and Salome are commissioned by a young man in white robes to proclaim the resurrection. Luke names Mary Magdalene, Joanna, Mary the mother of James, and the other women. These are commissioned by two men in dazzling clothes. Finally, in John's gospel, we find Mary Magdalene alone at the tomb. Two angels are in the place where the body of Jesus was laid. As Mary leaves the tomb, she meets Jesus, whom she does not recognize. It is in the way Jesus speaks her name that she recognizes the man she calls "teacher." It is Jesus who commissions her to proclaim the good news of the resurrection. The writings of the first-century Jewish historian, Flavius Josephus, proclaim that women were prohibited from testifying in court. Josephus writes, "But let not the testimony of women be admitted, on account of the levity and boldness of their sex."[1] The commentary on this quote reads, "The Pentateuch says not a word about the exclusion of women as witnesses in courts of justice. It is very probable, however, that this was the practice of the Jews in the days of Josephus."[2] Josephus is said to have been born in 37 C.E. and died in the year 100 C.E., at the same time as the Christian church was developing and the gospels were being written. Jesus, as recorded by the gospel writers, seems not to believe that women are too bold and cheerful to testify to the resurrection.

The *New Webster's Dictionary of the English Language* defines the word *apostle* as "one sent forth, a messenger."[3] "In the Pauline letters, the place where the term occurs most frequently in the New Testament, it means primarily one who has seen the risen Lord and has been commissioned to proclaim the resurrection." (NAB) *The New International Dictionary of the Bible* declares apostles were the "primary witnesses of the resurrection of Jesus."[4] Mary Magdalene is a disciple and an apostle. Much as twelve-year-old Lucinda Foot was denied admission to Yale University because of her gender, Mary Magdalene has been denied admittance to the list of disciples and apostles because of her gender, as have the other women who were followers of Jesus, ministered to him and witnessed the resurrection.

Paul uses the following arguments to defend himself as an apostle. In First Corinthians 9:1, Paul asks, "Am I not free? Am I not an apostle? Have I not seen Jesus our Lord?" (NRSV) Mary Magdalene can make the same argument. In Matthew 28:9, Jesus greets Mary Magdalene and the other Mary. They are commissioned by Jesus and by an angel to tell the good news of the resurrection. They are sent forth;

---

1 Flavius Josephus, *The Complete Works of Josephus,* trans. Wm. Whiston (Grand Rapids: Kregel Publications 1981), 97.

2 *Ibid.*

3 *New Webster's Dictionary of the English Language* (1981), s.v. "apostle."

4 *The New International Dictionary of the Bible* (1987), s.v. "apostle."

they are messengers. In First Corinthians 15:3–9, Paul pleads, "For I handed on to you as of first importance what I in turn had received: that Christ died for our sins in accordance with the scriptures, and that he was buried, and that he was raised on the third day in accordance with the scriptures, and that he appeared to Cephas, then to the twelve. Then he appeared to more than five hundred brothers at one time, most of whom are still alive, though some have died. Then he appeared to James, then to all the apostles, last of all, as to one untimely born, he appeared also to me." (NRSV) Paul does not seem to be aware it was not Peter (Cephas) who was the first to experience the risen Christ but the women who went to prepare the body of Jesus. Before the gospels had even been written, the importance of the women in the resurrection event had been diminished.

Who are all the apostles Paul speaks of? Did he include the women who were part of the group that ministered to Jesus? In Galatians 1:11–12, Paul states, "For I want you to know, brothers and sisters, that the gospel that was proclaimed by me is not of human origins; for I did not receive it from a human source, nor was I taught it, but I received it through a revelation of Jesus Christ." (NRSV) Paul argues for his own discipleship based on his experience of the risen Christ. All four gospels explicitly state that Mary Magdalene did not receive the good news of the resurrection from a human source. If every argument and plea Paul makes is valid as proof of the apostleship of Paul, it is equally valid for Mary Magdalene and the other women who were at the tomb on the morning of the resurrection. Paul says, "Have I not seen the risen Lord?" In Mark 6:7–13, Matthew 10:5–15, and Luke 6:12–16, the twelve are commissioned to proclaim that the reign of God is near. In Matthew, Mark, Luke and John, Mary Magdalene is commissioned to proclaim the nearness of the risen Christ.

Many stories which have no basis in biblical text have sprung up around Mary Magdalene over the years. She has been equated to the woman caught in adultery; however, there is no indication in the text that she was that woman. She has also been equated to the sinful woman who washes Jesus' feet in the gospel of Luke, but she is not. Nowhere in the Bible is Mary Magdalene called a prostitute. Luke 8:2 says seven demons had gone out of her, not that she was a prostitute. Mark 1:23 records the story of a man with an unclean spirit. His unclean spirit is not equated to prostitution. Likewise, the men, in the Gospel of Matthew, who live in the tombs of Gadarene, are said to be demoniacs. Their unclean spirits are not equated with prostitution or any other sexual activity. Mary Magdalene was a member of the inner circle of Jesus' disciples. She was very close to Jesus and was an apostle. Of that there can be no doubt. In Luke, the angel reminds the women that Jesus had taught them, "the Son of Man must be handed over to sinners, and be crucified, and on the third day rise again." (NRSV) Obviously, the women were among the inner circle of disciples being taught by Jesus.

The resurrection story recorded in the Gospel of John presents a new element in the last hours of Jesus' life. Mary Magdalene is still the first person at the tomb and is commissioned to proclaim the resurrection to the other disciples. However, the writer of the Gospel of John adds a scene in which the disciple whom Jesus loved and Peter race to the tomb after Mary has told them that Jesus' body is not there. It is this disciple whom Jesus loved who is the first to believe. It is also the disciple whom Jesus loved who stands with the women at the foot of Jesus' cross. If the narrator of the Gospel of John is the disciple whom Jesus loved, s/he is the only gospel writer who records this disciple reclining on Jesus' "breast" at the last supper, present at the crucifixion or being the first to believe in the resurrection.

Who was the disciple whom Jesus loved? Jesus was crucified sometime between 29 and 33 C.E. The Gospel of John was written between 90 and 120 C.E. *Moses Creighton* online states that the lifespan for a man in ancient Rome was between 20 and 40 years.[5]

---

[5] Bruce J. Malian, "New Testament Course Book," *Moses Creighton,* September 25, 2013. http://www.mosescreighton.edu/malian/ntstudy/ntcourse/slide14.html.

Thus, it is highly unlikely that the narrator of the Gospel of John was the disciple whom Jesus loved.

John 11:5 says that Jesus loved Martha, Mary and Lazarus. It was in the way Jesus said her name that Mary Magdalene recognized Jesus. What if Mary Magdalene was the beloved disciple? Several early Christian writings which did not become part of our biblical canon attest to the importance of Mary Magdalene. "*The Gospel of Mary* depicts Mary Magdalene (never recognized as an apostle by the orthodox) as the one favored with visions and insight that far surpass Peter's. *The Dialogue of the Savior* praises her not only as a visionary, but as the apostle who excels all the rest. She is the 'woman who knew the All.'"[6] In *The Gospel of Philip,* the male disciples ask Jesus why he loves Mary more than all of them. It also calls her his companion and says that he kissed her often.

Why has Mary been vilified and denied? Because some do not want to accept her importance as a disciple and companion of Jesus. As long as she remains a prostitute, her spiritual maturity and importance are diminished. To illustrate how charged this issue is: I was talking with a friend about Mary when her husband asked, "You know she was a prostitute, don't you?" My response was, "The Bible never says she was a prostitute. That doctrine wasn't developed until the middle ages." Before I could explain further, he waved his hands in the air and told his wife they were leaving. She later told me he muttered "She was a prostitute" all the way home.

An icon of Mary Magdalene hangs in my office. Part of the quote on the back of that print reads, "As women reclaim their ancient rights in the church, Mary Magdalene challenges all Christians to reexamine their cultural prejudices about gender and leadership."[7] The verses that tell the story of Mary Magdalene illustrate the commissioning of women.

---

6 Elaine Pagels, *The Gnostic Gospels* (New York: Random House, 1979), 22.

7 Bridge Building Images, Inc., *Saint Mary Magdalene.* Commissioned by Grace Cathedral, San Francisco, 1989.

Where to Find the Story of Peter's Wife and Mother-in-Law

Peter was a disciple of Jesus. He is, perhaps, the most well-known of the disciples, with the exception of Mary Magdalene. Peter had a wife and a mother-in-law. He left his fishing business to travel around the country and follow Jesus. Did he also leave his wife, or was she among the group of women who traveled with Jesus? If she was not with the disciples traveling with Jesus, how did she survive?

In First Corinthians 9:5, Paul asks, "Do we not have the right to be accompanied by a believing wife, as do the other apostles and the brothers of the Lord and Cephas?" (NRSV) This is all we know of Peter's wife, but her mother is mentioned in Mark 1:29–31, Matthew 8:14–15 and Luke 4:38–39. In Matthew 4:18–22, Jesus calls four male disciples. The women in the lives of these men must have been profoundly affected by the sudden departure of their husbands, fathers, sons and brothers. These four men no longer worked as fishermen because they left to follow Jesus.

Peter's Mother-in-Law Tells Her Story

> "He left his fishing business to fish for people? What does that mean?" (Peter's mother-in-law upon hearing that Peter had left to follow Jesus. Imaginative reconstruction of Matthew 4:29)

Peter must have heard that I was very ill. He brought Jesus home. I was furious with Peter and with this man, Jesus! I did not understand how Peter could leave my daughter and his fishing business to follow this itinerant teacher. And it wasn't just Peter. Andrew, Peter's brother, quit fishing, and so had Salome's sons James and John. Zebedee just sat in the boat mending his nets and let them go, and Jesus encouraged them? Fishing for people, indeed!

I expected Jesus to be like the other men who claimed to be prophets. They wandered around the country or led people out into the wilderness, trying to raise an army to overthrow the Romans. Jesus was nothing like I expected. He seemed to have a genuine concern for me. Most men would not talk to women they did not know, especially a sick woman. They were afraid they would be polluted. Jesus reached his hand out and touched me! I heard that he held unconventional ideas about many things he considered unfair. He touched me, without any apparent concern of becoming polluted. He touched me, an old, sick woman, on the Sabbath. I felt better immediately, physically and emotionally. I was not angry anymore. I got up and ministered to Jesus, the exceptional, kind, fearless teacher.

Observations on Peter's Mother-in-Law

We know that Peter's mother-in-law was sick. Jesus healed her. She got up and served the group Peter brought to her home. What we are *not* taught is that the Greek word *diakonia* is translated "to serve" or "to wait on" when it is applied to women. When the same word is applied to men, it is translated "deacon," and when angels are the subject, the word is translated "minister." Big difference! "Until recently, translators and most commentators understood these words as referring to Christian ministry when applied to men, to table service when applied to women."[8] Our understanding of the role of women as disciples of Jesus would be so different if the final sentence in the story of Peter's mother-in-law read: *then the fever left her and she became a deacon.*

Webster's New Collegiate Dictionary defines "deacon" as a servant or minister.[9] "Some English versions translate the verb designating her actions as 'serve,' which is acceptable as long as the same translation has been used for the word in its first appearance in the story in Mark 1:13, but some of those translations render the first occurrence as 'the angels *ministered* to him.' Translating the same Greek word as 'minister' when angels are the subject but 'serve' when a woman is the

8 *Dictionary of Feminist Theologies* (1996), s.v. "Diakonia."

9 *Webster's New Collegiate Dictionary,* 2nd ed., s.v. "deacon."

subject downplays her action. The author of Mark, by using the same word for the action of angels and the action of the healed woman, evidently equated their level of service to Jesus. What the angels were able to do for Jesus in the wilderness, the woman whose fever has fled does for him in her home."[10] This unnamed woman, known only by the name of a man in her family, demonstrates, in her action of service and ministry, a model for female deacons for today's church. "By the time that Mark and so all the gospel writers wrote, deacon would have been a loaded word, indicating an office in the church."[11]

Where to Find the Stories of Mary and Martha of Bethany

The stories of Mary and Martha of Bethany cannot be separated. They shared a home with their brother Lazarus and a friendship with Jesus. Unfortunately, these sisters suffered the same fate as other pairs of women in the Bible in that their relationship has been interpreted as adversarial. They are found in Luke 10:38–42, John 11:1–46; and 12:1–8.

Mary of Bethany Tells Her Story

> "If you would have been here, my brother would not have died." (Mary speaking to Jesus in John 11:32)

Jesus loved us and we loved him. He was a guest in our home many times. Martha and I lived with our brother Lazarus. I cherished the times Jesus was in our home. I could sit and listen to him for hours. He treated women so differently than the other men we knew. My sister is a fabulous host and a perfectionist. I was not much help to her when Jesus was visiting. She got quite irritated with me because I was not helping her. Jesus, as he always did, tried to comfort Martha.

---

[10] Newsom and Ringe, *op. cit.*, 267.

[11] Nancy Corran, written message to author, July 2011.

He acknowledged us among his followers and wanted her to relax and enjoy the company in her home. He wanted her to learn from him, like the rest of us, rather than work as hard as she did.

When our brother got sick, we sent for Jesus. We knew how healing his presence would be, and we knew how much Jesus loved Lazarus. We also knew it would be dangerous for Jesus to come to Bethany. Bethany is just two miles from Jerusalem. There are some in Jerusalem who are afraid of the momentum surrounding his movement. When Jesus finally did arrive, it was too late for our brother. He had died. Martha went out to meet Jesus. I stayed in the house with those who had come to comfort us.

When Martha ran back into the house to get me, she seemed changed. She told me that Jesus wanted to see me. I ran to him. I know it sounded like an accusation, but I said to Jesus, "If you would have been here, my brother would not have died." I could see that Jesus was very upset. He asked where we had taken Lazarus.

When we arrived at the cave, Jesus began to cry. What happened next can only be described as a miracle. Jesus asked that the stone which covered the mouth of the cave be removed. Martha tried to stop him. Lazarus had been dead for four days, and the smell would be overwhelming. Jesus looked intently into Martha's eyes and reminded her of their conversation and her declaration of faith in him. Then, the stone was removed and Jesus said a prayer for all to hear. It was a prayer like I had never heard before. Jesus was not asking God to give him anything. He thanked God for having heard him. He said he knew God always heard him. He said he wanted those standing around to know that God had sent him. Then he called my brother, and my brother walked out of the tomb. Many of the people who were there believed that Jesus was the Messiah, but some of them conspired with the Pharisees against Jesus.

It was not safe for Jesus after that. He could not walk around openly. We invited him to our home for a dinner in his honor. Of course, Martha, ever the perfect host, served a wonderful meal. I wanted to do something special for this amazing friend of ours. I took an expensive, aromatic ointment that I had been saving and rubbed it on Jesus' feet. The whole house was scented with the ointment. Judas was short-tempered and complained that the ointment should have been sold and the money given to the poor. Jesus told him to leave me alone. He knew that what I had done was out of love for him. He was aware there were some powerful men who wanted to kill him.

Martha of Bethany Tells Her Story

> "I believe you are the Christ, the son of God, who is coming into the world." (Martha's profession of faith in Jesus found in John 11:27, similar to Peter's confession in Matthew 16:16)

I was so glad to see Jesus, but I was so sad he had not gotten to us in time to help my brother. I knew if he had come earlier, my brother would not have died, and I told him so. He began talking to me about the resurrection on the last day. Thinking about the last day was no consolation to me. My brother was dead, and I was heartbroken now. I said I knew he would rise at the final resurrection. Then, Jesus said something which astounded me but which I think I had known since I met him. He said, "I am the resurrection and the life. Those who believe in me, even though they die, will live, and everyone who lives and believes in me will never die." (NRSV) Then he asked me if I believed him. I knew in that moment who my friend Jesus really was. I said, "Yes, I believe you are the Messiah." I ran to get Mary.

I loved having Jesus as a guest in my home. We were his friends and his disciples. Mary would sit for long hours talking to Jesus. I must confess, I did get upset with her, but Jesus calmed me down. He knew I made a lot of extra work for myself when he and our other friends were there. He affirmed Mary's place as one of his disciples, and he gave me permission to relax my hosting responsibilities to join the conversation. Jesus was so sensitive. Men simply assumed women would work hard serving them, but Jesus knew it was better for a woman to take the opportunity to learn rather than spend endless hours serving the men.

Observations on the Sisters Martha and Mary

The author of Luke presents the story of Martha and her sister, Mary, as an antagonistic relationship. Mary sits quietly at the feet of Jesus while Martha is busy preparing the meal for the family and the guests. *The 1965 Oxford Annotated Bible* says this about the story of Martha, Mary and Jesus. "With delicate ambiguity Jesus rebuked Martha's choice of values; a simple meal (one dish) is sufficient for hospitality. Jesus approved Mary's preference for listening to his teaching as contrasted with Martha's unneeded acts of hospitality."[12] Yet the same volume says of Lot's offer to hand his daughters over to the mob of rapists outside his door, "Once a guest had eaten in his house, Lot had to obey the law of oriental hospitality which guaranteed protection. Thus, his proposal to hand over his daughters showed his determination to put first his obligation as a host."[13] What about a rebuke of Lot's choice of values? Was the rape of Lot's virgin daughters not *unneeded* hospitality? Why is Martha rebuked for striving to obey the law of hospitality and Lot is not rebuked for offering his virgin daughters to rapists?

The New American Bible does not address the issue of hospitality in this story but rather the position of Mary at Jesus feet. "It is remarkable for first-century Palestinian Judaism that a woman would assume the posture of a disciple at the master's feet and it reveals a characteristic attitude of Jesus toward women in this gospel." (NAB)

The New Oxford Annotated states, "This enigmatic account affirms the importance of listening to Jesus and at the same time the account shows Jesus' openness to and acceptance of women among his

---

12 May and Metzger, *op. cit.*

13 *Ibid.*

followers." (NRSV) The three times we see Mary in the gospels she is sitting at Jesus feet, falling at his feet, or anointing his feet.

The commentators of *The Oxford Annotated* make the assumption that the many things Martha is anxious and troubled about is the food she is preparing. But the text says it is the serving which distracts Martha. As in the case of Peter's mother-in-law, the serving by which Martha is distracted is *diakonia*. Was she simply serving a meal, ministering or performing the function of a deacon? Both sisters are behaving in culturally inappropriate manners. Mary is sitting at the feet of Jesus in the position of a rabbinic disciple. Unfortunately, the questions she might have asked Jesus about his teachings have not been recorded. She is, however, praised for her choice. Martha, who seems to be in charge of the household, is serving or ministering. Is the apparent rebuke of Martha intended to inform female readers that the *diakonia* which Martha is performing is less acceptable for women than sitting quietly at the feet of Jesus? Is the writer of the Gospel of Luke, written some fifty years after the life of Jesus, attempting to put words into the mouth of Jesus which distorts "Jesus' openness to and acceptance of women among his followers?" (NRSV) Jesus treated women and all people as equals. It does not make sense that Jesus would rebuke one sister for culturally inappropriate behavior and not the other. Both Mary in her position at Jesus' feet, and Martha, in her attitude of service, are models of true discipleship.

Martha says to Jesus in John 11:27, "I believe that you are the Messiah, the Son of God, the One coming into the world." Similarly, Peter in Matthew 16:16 says, "You are the Messiah, the Son of the living God." In Mark 8:29 and Luke 9:20, Peter makes similar confessions. Jesus says these confessions are the rock upon which he will build his church. The confession of Martha is of equal significance to that of Peter. Her confession and that of Peter are the rock upon which the church is built, whether the words are uttered by a man or a woman. "Martha does not get the same acknowledgement as Peter. It is that passage about Peter in Matthew that is said to commission

Peter as the first pope. If that is so, then Martha should also have been pope since she meets that same criterion, gender notwithstanding."[14]

Where to Find the Story of Salome, the Mother of the Sons of Thunder

Salome is visible four times in the Bible: in Mark 15:40–41; 16:1, Matthew 20:20–23 and 27:55–56. In each of her appearances, she demonstrates courage. She is at the crucifixion of Jesus. She is among the women who come to anoint Jesus' body, and she approaches Jesus on behalf of her sons to request a place of honor for them in the realm she believes Jesus is establishing.

Salome Tells Her Story

> "Command that these two sons of mine may sit, one at your right and one at your left when you come into power." (Salome's request of Jesus in Matthew 20:21)

I am Salome. I am the mother of the sons of Zebedee, also called the sons of thunder. Jesus gave my sons that name because of my commanding personality. I was respectful but not shy when I asked Jesus to announce that my sons were to sit at his right and left sides when he established his empire. I was sure that as revolutionary as Jesus' thinking was, he would lead a new realm. It was not to be. I was with the women who stood fearlessly at the crucifixion of Jesus with Mary Magdalene, Mary Jesus' mother, her sister, Joanna, Mary the mother of James, Susanna and so many of the other women. I also returned to anoint the body of Jesus.

Observations on Salome

Jesus called the sons of Salome and Zebedee "the sons of thunder." I am sure that their mother is the thunder about whom Jesus was speaking.

---

[14] Nancy Corran, written message to author, July 2011.

Zebedee is mentioned four times in the gospels. Two of those times Zebedee is sitting passively in his boat mending nets as his sons leave him to follow Jesus. Nothing else is told about Zebedee. I used to think Jesus called James and John the sons of thunder because of their personalities. Now I am more inclined to think that the personality of their mother was the "thunder" to which Jesus referred. The sons were in hiding when Jesus was being crucified, but Salome was at the foot of the cross with the other women.

The *Illustrated Dictionary and Concordance of the Bible* calls Salome "the wife of Zebedee and mother of apostles James and John."[15] In contrast to the passivity of Zebedee, Salome approaches Jesus to ask for positions of importance for her sons at Jesus' right and left hand. She is among the courageous women mentioned at the crucifixion and at the tomb. She is commissioned in Mark by a young man in white robes to proclaim the resurrection. The women followers of Jesus were the first to proclaim the resurrection to the unbelieving male disciples. They were commissioned by angels and by Jesus himself. It is apparent from the biblical text that women were among those Jesus taught about the resurrection. In Mark 16:7, a young man tells the women that they will see Jesus, "Just as he told you." (NRSV) In Matthew 28:6, an angel tells the women, "He has been raised, as he said." (NRSV) And in Luke 24:6, it is two men who remind the women, "Remember how he told you, while he was still in Galilee, that the Son of Man must be handed over to sinners, and be crucified, and on the third day rise again." (NRSV) In all three incidences, the women are reminded of what Jesus had taught them.

Where to Find the Story of the Disciples on the Road to Emmaus

The final story about the women who were friends and disciples of Jesus occurs after his resurrection. Although we are never told the

[15] *Illustrated Dictionary & Concordance of the Bible* (1986), s.v. "Salome."

gender of the couple traveling home from Jerusalem, I believe it is very likely that one of them was a woman. Their story is found in Luke 24:13–35.

> ***The Couple on the Road to Emmaus Tell Their Story***
> "Didn't our hearts burn within us while he talked to us on the road?" (The couple talking about their experience with Jesus in Luke 24:32)

We were heartbroken on our way home to Emmaus after the crucifixion of our friend! A strange man approached us and walked along with us. He asked what we were talking about and why we were so sad. We found it hard to believe there was anyone who did not know what had happened to Jesus. Cleopas told him about Jesus, the prophet who would liberate Israel. He had been killed by the powerful men of the Roman occupation government and the Sanhedrin. Some of the women in our group told us about their vision at the tomb when they had gone to anoint Jesus' body. The women were convinced Jesus was alive.

This man called us fools because we did not believe the women. Then he began to interpret our Scriptures as they pertained to the messiah. We invited him into our home because it was almost evening. When we were ready to eat, he blessed the bread and gave it to us. In that moment, we recognized our friend. How many times had we sat at the table with him as he blessed the bread?

We could not contain our joy. We practically ran all the way back to Jerusalem to tell our group that the women were right. Jesus was alive, and we had seen him.

Observations on the Couple on the Road to Emmaus

The distance from Jerusalem to Emmaus was approximately seven miles. Who were the two on the road to Emmaus? Luke 24:13 says,

"Two of them." Two of whom? The disciples? They were not members of the eleven, because as soon as they recognized Jesus, they returned to the eleven to relate their experience. One of them was named Cleopas. The *Illustrated Dictionary & Concordance of the Bible* says that Cleopas is "sometimes identified with Clopas, the husband of Mary who stood by the cross with the mother of Jesus."[16] The two of them seem to share a home. They invite Jesus to stay with them and share a meal. They were close enough to the eleven that the first thing they do is rush back to them. We know there were women in the company of Jesus because they tell him some of the women of their company said that Jesus was alive. It is probable that the two on the road to Emmaus were a husband-and-wife team who were disciples of Jesus. Later, Priscilla and Aquila were a team in the founding and development of the early church.

Conclusion

Evidence abounds if we are simply willing to look past the way the Bible has previously been interpreted. Women were there. They were part of the group that followed and supported Jesus and his message. Mary Magdalene was important enough to the early church that the *Gospel of Mary*, written between 120 to 180 C.E., was written in the name of this woman. The Gospel of John tells us that Jesus loved the sisters Mary and Martha. Mary is depicted as sitting at the feet of Jesus in the attitude of discipleship, while Martha performs the function of a deacon. We do not know the stories of Joanna, Susanna, Salome, or the other women named and unnamed. But it is the women who demonstrate true discipleship during the final moments of Jesus' life and beyond.

---

16 *Illustrated Dictionary & Concordance of the Bible* (1986), s.v. "Clopas."

Chapter Six

Women in Jesus' Parables and Public Life

Jesus encountered many women in his public life: the woman accused of adultery, the widow of Nain, the woman with the flow of blood, Jairus' daughter, the woman who anointed Jesus' head, the woman who anointed Jesus' feet, the crippled woman, the poor widow, the Canaanite woman and her daughter, the woman at the well and all those unnamed, uncounted women in the crowds who are acknowledged only by the dismissive phrase "not counting women and children."

Each of the four gospels records an event where large numbers of people were fed. The story of the loaves and the fishes is found in Matthew 14:14–21, John 6:8–20, Mark 6:32–44 and Luke 9:10–17. Matthew's version is the only one with the phrase, "not counting women and children." That phrase is at the center for understanding the feeding miracles associated with the large gatherings where Jesus taught the crowds.

Women know that women who can afford it do not leave home without snacks for their children. In Jesus' day, the snacks were probably dry fish, dates, unleavened bread and an animal skin filled with goat's milk. Today, the snacks may be goldfish crackers, cheese sticks, fruit roll-ups and drink boxes. It happens every day at parks and playgrounds where women and their children gather. The snacks are unpacked and shared. The leftovers to be packed up seem to be more than when the sharing began.

John 6:8–20 tells of a boy who gave Jesus two small pieces of fish and five small loaves of bread, undoubtedly packed for him by his mother that morning. Jesus prayed over the food and had the people sit down. Remember that people here means *men,* not *men, women and children.*

Commentators have different interpretations of this story. Some say that it is an allusion to the stories of the Hebrew prophets Elijah and Elisha. Others say that it is a prediction of the Eucharist. But, this is a story of the preparedness of the women—women who were part of the crowd but were not counted, women who ministered to and provided for Jesus, women who were the female disciples, not counted as disciples. Matthew 27:55 says, "Many women were also there, looking on from a distance; they had followed Jesus from Galilee and had provided for him." (NRSV) The people sat down and the women pulled out the snacks they packed for themselves and their children and fed the crowds. Does this make the feeding of the thousands any less of a miracle? No. It is just a different way to understand the miracle and the profound effect the person Jesus had on people.

It is not surprising that the feeding of the thousands looked like a miracle to the male disciples. They were notorious for being unprepared. A notable example is the journey from Judea to Galilee recorded in John 4:1–42. The male disciples knew they were going on a trip, but they packed neither food nor water. It is a good thing for our next woman they were so ill prepared. If they had been prepared, she would have missed her chance to have a deeply theological conversation with Jesus. She would have missed her chance to be the first person to evangelize, to preach, and to convert people to faith in Jesus.

There was a deep division between the Judeans and the Samaritans. According to *The Westminster Historical Atlas to the Bible*, "On most of his trips to Jerusalem, Jesus probably followed the usual Galilean custom, journeying down the Jordan Valley on the East side of the river, crossing the river near Jericho."[1] There had been animosity between the Samaritans and the Judeans for more than seven hundred years. The Judeans worshipped God in the temple in Jerusalem while the Samaritans worshipped God in their temple on Mount Gerizim. It is about their theological differences that the woman questions Jesus.

The Samaritan Woman at the Well Tells Her Story

> "Come see the man who told me all I ever did." (The woman at the well, preaching about Jesus to the people of her village in John 4:29)

I am a woman of Samaria, and I was the first to preach the good news of the coming of the Messiah to my people. It was the most amazing experience, and it changed my life forever. I had gone to Jacob's well at midday to draw water. It was a dangerous thing to do. Women usually go to the well in the morning or in the evening with other women, but I needed the water. A woman alone is never safe. There was a man at the well, a man of Judea. This was very unusual because the Judeans avoid Samaria. I was apprehensive. A woman alone can never be too careful. He asked me for a drink of water. I was shocked when he spoke to me. A Judean speaking

---

1 George Ernst Wright and Floyd Vivian Filson, eds., *The Westminster Historical Atlas to the Bible: Revised Edition* (Philadelphia: The Westminster Press, 1974), 94.

to a Samaritan woman in public is just not done. I was even more astonished that this man was asking me for a drink of water. Judeans view Samaritans with contempt and believe we are always ritually unclean. For him to drink from my jar would make him unclean also. So I asked him, "Why are you speaking to me? I am a woman and a Samaritan." His response was not at all what I expected. At first it was so difficult to understand. He said if I understood the gifts of God and who I was talking to, I would have asked him for a drink. He said he could give me "living water." He did not have anything in which to carry water, so I was confused about what he meant by that. I listened intently to what he had to say. Here was a man and a Judean engaging me in a meaningful conversation. He seemed to know everything about me. I asked him why the Judeans hated the Samaritans so much and why they insisted that God must be worshipped in Jerusalem and not on Mt. Gerizim, where Samaritans have always worshipped. He did not argue with me about our place of worship but instead spoke of worshipping God in Spirit and in Truth. "God," he declared, "is Spirit." I told him I knew the Messiah was coming, and he said, "I am he." I think I knew that was true even before he told me.

When his friends returned, I ran back into town to tell the people of my village about the coming of the Messiah. Many of the people believed my message and went out to the well to meet him. While I was gone, Jesus talked to his friends about me. I am sure they were shocked to find him talking to me, but they didn't say anything in my presence. He compared my preaching to the work of one who sows in the fields. He told his friends that the fields of Samaria were ready for harvest. He told them he sent them to reap where others had labored. They did not understand that he was talking about me. After all, in their eyes I was a despised, ritually unclean, Samaritan woman. But it was me. I sowed the word of truth in my town. I led people to believe in the Messiah. Jesus, the Messiah of God, had entrusted the truth of who he was to me, a woman.

Observations on the Woman at the Well

The woman at the well engages Jesus in an authentic theological discussion. This point is often overlooked because of the number of husbands she had had and the fact that she was living with a man who was not her husband. Jesus does not condemn her for her multiple husbands. He uses his understanding of her life circumstances as a vehicle to demonstrate his prophetic powers. According to the law recorded in Deuteronomy 24:1–4, it is the husband who initiates divorce, not the wife. If she were divorced five times, it would have been because five different men had divorced her or died, a particularly devastating circumstance for a woman in a culture where her worth was determined by her relationship to father, husband or sons. It may have been that this woman was caught in the law of Levirate marriage, as recorded in Deuteronomy 25:4–6. In Matthew 22:24–28, the Sadducees attempt to trick Jesus by asking him, at the resurrection, who would a woman "belong" to if she had been married to seven brothers.

The misconception about the character of the Samaritan woman is an example of the bias that has crept into our understanding of the text. I have heard it taught that this woman was a prostitute, although the text says nothing to that effect. It may be odd that she was at the well alone at midday, but there could be any number of explanations for her actions. Considering the positive reaction of the people in her village to her preaching about Jesus, it is very unlikely that she was a prostitute. I cannot imagine the people would believe in Jesus on the strength of the woman's testimony, as the text declares, if she were not a well-respected woman in the community. The Samaritan woman is the first to evangelize, the first to preach to the gentiles, long before Paul. She receives the good news of the great I AM directly from Jesus and rushes off to proclaim him to her village.

The commentary in *The New American Bible* says, "Talking with a woman: a religious and social restriction that Jesus is pictured treating as unimportant." (NAB) Jesus breaks religious and social restrictions by engaging this woman in a theological conversation. He is not constrained by the limits his culture would have put on his conversation with this supposedly ritually unclean, Samaritan woman. The woman herself notes the surprising nature of this conversation, as do the male disciples on their return, although they keep it to themselves. Jesus will not be bound by what is acceptable cultural behavior. He is revolutionary in his treatment of women. Just as Mary Magdalene is sent to proclaim the good news of the resurrection and "Martha proclaims Jesus as the Messiah,"[2] so this Samaritan woman proclaims Jesus as the Messiah.

It is while she is away, evangelizing her village, that Jesus talks to his disciples about the sower and the reaper. He compares the disciples to those who reap what others have sown. It is the Samaritan woman in her village who is the sower from whose labor the disciples profit.

Where to Find the Perplexing Story of the Anointing Woman

There are four gospel stories of Jesus being anointed by a woman. Are there four different women who anoint Jesus, or is there one woman whose story is told by four different gospel writers with four different agendas? She is found in Mark 14:3–9, Matthew 26:6–13, Luke 7:36–50 and John 12:1–7.

The anointing woman cannot tell her story. She never has a voice. We learn everything we know about her from Jesus and others who talk about her. The Gospel of Mark is believed to be the first gospel written. The date for the composition of this gospel is sometime around 70 C.E., making its composition some thirty or more years after the events of Jesus' life. Although the book is anonymous, church tradition attributes it to John Mark. John Mark is first mentioned in Acts 12:12 in connection to the church in his mother's home. The

---

2 Nancy Corran, written message to author, July 2011.

writer of the gospel of Mark tells us that Jesus is having dinner at the house of Simon the Leper. Lepers were ritually unclean. Leviticus 13:45–46 states, "The person who has the leprous disease shall wear torn clothes and let the hair of his head be disheveled; and he shall cover his upper lip and cry out, 'Unclean, unclean' as long as he has the disease; he is unclean. He shall live alone; his dwelling shall be outside the camp." (NRSV) For Jesus to be sharing a meal with a ritually unclean person would have been a very controversial event, unless Simon had been pronounced clean by a priest and the name Simon the Leper just stuck.

This is another instance when Jesus is pictured as breaking religious and social restrictions. In Mark's story, an unnamed woman breaks an alabaster jar of costly oil and pours it over the head of Jesus. There are many at the meal who are "indignant" and complain about the waste of the expensive oil. Jesus tells them to "Leave her alone." He then makes an astonishing prediction. Jesus says in Mark 14:9, "Truly I tell you, wherever the good news is proclaimed in the whole world, what she has done will be told in remembrance of her." (NRSV) I say "astonishing" because, as important as Jesus thought her actions were, the Gospel writers did not even record her name. It is also astonishing that later commentators are not concerned by the fact that her name was not recorded. What they are concerned with is the identity of Simon the Leper. This story is also told in Matthew 26. The footnote for Matthew 26:6 in *The Oxford Annotated Bible* states, "The identity of this Simon is unknown." (RSV) Simon was not the person whose actions were of significance to Jesus. I have never heard the gospel preached in memory of the nameless woman who anointed Jesus' head. *The New Oxford Annotated Bible* states, "*In remembrance of her*, perhaps an indication of the important place of women early in the formation of the Christian Church." (NRSV)

The woman who anointed Jesus' head was fulfilling the prophetic function of anointing a king much as Samuel anointed David.

"Anointing on the head is an act of great symbolic importance. To tend to someone's feet, as in Luke and John, is the act of a social inferior—a slave or a woman. But a host might anoint a guest's head as a sign of rejoicing. To anoint the head is also to call a person to God's service, to consecrate him or her for a special task. Prophets and priests were anointed, but, above all, prophets anointed those chosen to be king. So the unknown woman at Bethany was a prophet, fulfilling the prophetic function of choosing and empowering Jesus for his messianic role."[3] There are other female prophets noted in the Hebrew and Christian Scriptures: Miriam is called a prophet in Exodus 15:20; Deborah is named a prophet in Judges 4:4; Huldah in Second Kings 22:14; Noadiah in Nehemiah 6:14; and the unnamed wife of Isaiah in Isaiah 8:3. In the Christian Scriptures, Anna in Luke 2:36 and the four daughters of Philip in Acts 21:8 are also called prophets.

Both Matthew and Luke used Mark as one source for their Gospels. Matthew is true to his source, and in 26:6 he retells the story of the woman who anoints Jesus. It is not until the Gospel of Luke, written some ten to twenty years after Mark, that the anointing woman who anoints Jesus' feet in 7:36–50 becomes "sinful." Luke places Jesus in the home of Simon the Pharisee, not Simon the Leper. As noted above, the anointing of the feet would have been the culturally appropriate act of a woman or a slave, and the home of Simon the Pharisee would be a more culturally acceptable home in which Jesus would have a meal. Luke acknowledges that he was not an eyewitness to the ministry of Jesus in 1:2. Do we believe that there was another woman that anointed Jesus or that the story has been changed to fit what the author of the Gospel of Luke thought was culturally appropriate? Was it difficult for the author of Luke, writing eighty or ninety years after the fact, to believe that the anointing woman was a prophet? It appears that

---

3 Joanna Dewey, "The Gospel of Mark," in *Searching the Scriptures: A Feminist Commentary*, ed. Elizabeth Schussler Fiorenza, 470–509 (New York: Crossroad, 1994), 501.

the church had already begun to close down the openness to women that Jesus demonstrated in his lifetime!

The Gospel of John was written even later, sometime between 90 and 100 C.E. In John's version of the story, it is Mary, the sister of Martha and Lazarus of Bethany, who anoints Jesus. She also dries Jesus' feet with her hair as the "sinful" woman did in Luke. Are these four stories about four different women or the story of one woman? What are the similarities in these stories? In the gospels of Matthew, Mark and John, Jesus is said to be in Bethany. Luke just says "a city." Matthew, Mark and Luke describe the container as being alabaster. John just calls it "a liter." The content is perfumed oil, except in Luke it is called "ointment." Mark and Matthew give the time as two days before Passover, Luke doesn't say, and John thinks it is six days before Passover. The host is Simon the Leper in Mark and Matthew, Simon the Pharisee in Luke, Martha, Mary and Lazarus in John. In Mark, some of the guests are reported to be indignant and infuriated with the woman. In Matthew, it is the male disciples who are indignant. They complain about the waste and want to give the money to the poor. In John, it is only Judas who is upset. In Mark, Matthew and John, Jesus tells them to leave her alone and uses the opportunity to teach about doing good for the poor and to predict his death. He says she has anointed him for burial. Luke has an entirely different agenda, putting words in Jesus' mouth which teach about faith and the forgiveness of sins.

The woman who anointed Jesus was obviously important enough for her story to be recorded in all four gospels. We have not been taught about the woman, but we do know what Jesus thought of her contribution. Sister Miriam Therese Winter believes there are three women who anoint Jesus: one who anoints his head, recorded in Mark and Matthew, and two who anoint his feet (the woman called "a sinner" in the Gospel of Luke, and Mary of Bethany in the Gospel of John). We do not know for sure because, except for Mary of Bethany, no other information is recorded about the woman in whose memory the gospel is to be proclaimed.

Where to Find Anna the Prophet

Anna is called a prophet in the second chapter of Luke. The future of Jesus is the subject of her prophetic powers in this verse.

Anna the Prophet Tells Her Story

> "This child will be the redemption of Jerusalem." (Anna the prophet proclaims about Jesus in Luke 2:38)

I am from the line of Zilpah, handmaid of Leah and concubine of Jacob, from the tribe of their son Asher. I was eighty-four years old when Mary brought her son to the Temple for consecration to God as our law required. Exodus 13:2 states, "Consecrate to me all the first born; whatever is the first to open the womb among the Israelites, of human beings and animals, is mine." (NRSV) I am called a prophet. I have lived, prayed and fasted in the temple in the Court of the Women since my husband died when I was very young. I knew the moment I saw Mary and her beautiful son that he was the One Promised. I praised God and told all who would listen this is the Promised One who will redeem Israel.

Observations on Anna the Prophet

Because Jesus' genealogy is also traced back through Jacob, the Prophet Anna would have been a distant relative of Jesus. Unlike Philip's four prophetic daughters, Anna's voice is recorded as she prophesies Jesus as the redemption of Israel.

Where to Find the Story of the Woman Accused of Adultery

The woman accused of adultery is found only in the gospel of John: 8:2–11. She is not named. There is no reason to believe that she was Mary Magdalene.

The Woman Accused of Adultery Tells Her Story

"No one, sir." (The woman's response to Jesus question, "Is no one left to condemn you?" in John 8:11)

I was caught with a man who was not my husband. I thought we would both be killed as the law requires, but I was the only one the scribes and the Pharisees dragged away. They took me to the Temple. Their goal was to humiliate me before they stoned me to death. They made me stand in front of them. A teacher was there, and they asked him what they should do with me. I was sure he would say, "Kill her; it is what the law requires." But he did not. His face became very thoughtful, and he bent down and wrote something on the ground. Then he straightened and gave me a look which calmed my fearful soul, but his words terrified me. He told the men that the one among them who had never committed a sin should throw the first stone. I was afraid that was just the excuse these self-righteous men wanted. I saw one young man seize a stone to throw, but an older man grabbed his arm and took the stone away from him. As the men began to leave, my savior bent down to write in the dirt again. I did not know what to do, so I just stood there. When all the men had gone, my savior stood up and asked me if there was anyone left to condemn me. "No one," I said. He told me he did not condemn me either and instructed me to go on my way and not sin again.

Observations on the Woman Accused of Adultery

This woman accused of adultery has often been identified as Mary Magdalene or as the sinful woman who anoints Jesus' feet. There is no biblical evidence to suggest that she was either of those two women. She may have been a woman who was being raped when discovered or a divorced woman who had remarried. The laws to which the scribes and the Pharisees refer are found in Leviticus 20:10 and Deuteronomy 22:23–24. Leviticus says, "If a man commits adultery with the wife of his neighbor, both the adulterer and the adulteress shall be put to death." (NRSV) Deuteronomy states, "If there is a young woman, a virgin already engaged to be married, and a man meets her in the town and lies with her, you shall bring both of them to the gate of that town and stone them to death, the young woman because she did not cry for help in the town and the man because he violated his neighbor's wife. So shall you purge the evil from your midst." (NRSV) There are other provisions in Deuteronomy for consequences to both man and woman if a man rapes an engaged woman outside of town or an unengaged woman. Why did the scribes and Pharisees not bring both the adulterer and the adulteress? Why is just the woman condemned? There is no double standard in the laws to which they refer. Is this situation similar to the practice commonly reported today in which a prostitute is arrested but her patron is not? According to Sienna Baskin, Esq., interim co-director of Sex Workers Project Urban Justice Center, "In New York City, prostitution arrests are about twice as frequent as patronizing arrests."[4]

In *The Women's Biblical Commentary*, Gail R. O'Day says this about the accused woman, the scribes and the Pharisees:

> A careful reading of this story shows that Jesus' focus is not on the woman alone but is evenly divided between the scribes and Pharisees and the woman. Jesus bends down and writes twice and twice stands to address his conversation partners. Indeed, what is striking about this story is that Jesus treats the woman as the social and human equal of the scribes and Pharisees. Jesus speaks to both sets of characters about sin. His words to the scribes and Pharisees, "Let anyone among you who is without sin be the first to throw a stone at her" envisions the past. The way the crowd has lived until this moment. His words to the woman, "Neither do I condemn you. Go your way and from now on do not sin again" envision

---

4 Sienna Baskin, written message to author, August 2012.

> the future, the way the woman could live from now on. Jesus invites both the scribes and the Pharisees and the woman to begin life anew in the present moment. They are invited to give up old ways and enter a new way of life.[5]

Similar to the story of the Samaritan woman at the well, the focus of this story has been on the sexuality of the woman and not the words and actions of Jesus. The agenda of the scribes and Pharisees was to trick Jesus. They were not concerned with fulfilling the law. They did not bring the woman's partner for condemnation and stoning. In John 8:15–16, Jesus is quoted as saying, "You judge by human standards; I judge no one. Yet even if I do judge, my judgment is valid; for it is not I alone who judge, but I and the Father who sent me." (NRSV) Jesus does not judge this woman based on unjust social structures which would have cost her her life. Rather, Jesus demonstrates justice in a manner not tied to the social structures which condemn the woman. Jesus does not treat the woman any differently than he treats her male accusers. Her sin is not greater than theirs. Perhaps Jesus was aware of stories that may have circulated about his mother's pregnancy before her marriage to Joseph. Perhaps he understood what the consequences could have been for his mother and himself. Perhaps his passion for justice for all people was based on his personal understanding of what unequal treatment could mean in the life of an individual.

Where to Find the Story of the Hemorrhaging Woman and the Twelve-Year-Old Girl

In Mark 5:25–43, Matthew 9:18–25 and Luke 8:41–56, we find two women's stories tied together, a twelve-year-old girl who is dying and a woman who has been hemorrhaging for twelve years. The woman has been hemorrhaging for as long as the little girl has been alive

[5] Newsom and Ringe, *op. cit.*, 297.

and thus has been ritually unclean. It should be noted that twelve is approximately the age at which a girl would begin menstruation and would thus become ritually unclean herself. The little girl does not speak in the gospels. We do not know her name, but we do know her father was named Jairus and that he was an official of the synagogue. The little girl is reported to be dead, but Jesus restores her to her family much the way the hemorrhaging woman is restored to her life as a member of her community.

The Hemorrhaging Woman Tells Her Story

> "If I but touch his clothes, I will be well." (The hemorrhaging woman says to herself in Mark 5:28)

I saw the crowd, so I knew He was near. I had lost all hope of ever being cured. It is a dreadful life to live as one impure for twelve long years. No one would touch me or anything I sat on or slept on. They would become unclean like me except they could bathe and be clean by evening. I was always unclean. I lived alone and could have no part in the community or the temple. It was a very lonely existence. I spent all I had on physician after physician and had not gotten any better, just poorer. I believed if I could just touch the fringe of His garment, I would be saved from this hemorrhage. It was taking a terrible risk going into the crowd in my state of pollution, but I was desperate. He was my last hope. I summoned all my courage, prayed no one recognized me, and headed straight for him. I was lucky. I got close enough to touch the fringe on his robe.

He spun around and demanded to know who touched him. The men with him seemed a little aggravated with his question. One of them said, "Come on, Jesus, you see this huge crowd pressing in on you, and you want to identify one person who touched you!" But he looked right into my eyes. I could feel in my body that something wonderful had happened to me, but I was still terrified. What had I been thinking? I, an unclean woman, had been so bold as to touch a man, and a Rabbi at that. My touch made this man unclean, and I was afraid of the consequences. This was no ordinary man. He smiled into my eyes and said, "Take heart." He called me "daughter" and told me to "take heart"—my faith made me well. It was the greatest day of my life. My health and my bond with the community were restored.

Observations on the Hemorrhaging Woman

Leviticus 15:25–30 prescribes the law for a woman who is hemorrhaging. She is unclean. The same is true when a woman menstruates. As long as she continues to hemorrhage, she is unclean, not allowed to participate in the ritual life of the community, and not allowed to touch or be touched by other members of the community. She will defile anyone who touches her.

Jesus, however, does not condemn the woman for breaking the purity code or for touching him and making him ritually impure. Instead, he praises her for her faith. Jesus demonstrates his contempt for social structures that punish the sick and stigmatize the natural, which includes God-given functions of a woman's body. Jesus would show the same contempt for present-day social structures which blame the victims of rape, domestic violence, sexual harassment and poverty. Jesus' passion for justice would not allow for discrimination or unjust social structures of any kind.

Where to Find the Story of the Gentile Woman

She is sometimes called the Syrophoenician woman. Her name, the name of her daughter and the nature of the disease from which the daughter suffered have not been remembered. What we do know about her is that she taught Jesus a lesson in compassion. She also generated in him a new perspective on his grander mission to the gentiles, not just his own religious community. She can be found in Mark 7:24–29 and Matthew 15:22–28.

The Gentile Woman Tells Her Story

> "Even the dogs eat the scraps under the table." (The woman's response to Jesus' insinuation that she and her daughter are dogs in Mark 7:28)

My little daughter was sick, so sick, and I was desperate to help her. I heard of a man who was a great healer, but he was in Galilee. I could not leave my child to go down there or take her that far. Then word spread that this healer was in the area of Tyre, which was a much shorter trip for me. I found out where he was staying. I was very frightened. The healer was Judean, and the Judeans view anyone who is not of their tribe with contempt. I was desperate to help my child, so I humbled myself and threw myself at this man's feet. I begged him to help my child. I told him she was possessed by a demon. He turned cold eyes on me and asked, "Is it right to give dogs the food of the children?" He called me a dog! I was shocked! I couldn't believe this man was calling me and my precious child "dogs." That was so insulting! "Well," I snapped, "Even the dogs get to eat the scraps that fall from the children's table." His whole attitude changed. His eyes softened, and he spoke kindly to me. "Your faith is great," he said. "Go home; your little girl is well." I ran all the way home. My baby girl was sitting up in her bed smiling at me. My faith in the goodness of this man had changed our lives forever.

Observations on the Gentile Woman

Letty Russell called this story "Jesus caught with his compassion down."[6] What is really going on here? Is Jesus rude to her because she is a gentile? He did not speak harshly to the centurion in Matthew 8:5–13 who was also a gentile. Instead, Jesus praised the centurion for his great faith and told those around them that nowhere in Israel had he found such faith. Jesus tells the woman he will not help her

---

5 Letty Russell, personal communication to author, July 2001.

because he was sent only to the lost sheep of the house of Israel. The centurion receives no such rebuke. *The Women's Biblical Commentary* says this about the gentile woman "Her very action, daring to approach a strange man on behalf of her family, was an unconventional and, evidently to Jesus, unacceptable act. The protection and care of an honorable family were the responsibility of the father or other senior male relative."[7] Jesus, however, continually demonstrates his unconventional attitudes and actions, especially as associated with women and the ritually unclean or societal outcasts. This gentile woman understands Jesus' mission better than Jesus. Her argument helps Jesus understand his universal mission and not just his mission to Israel.

The final three women in the public life of Jesus are old, silent and poor. Observations of all three women will follow their stories.

The Widow of Nain Tells Her Story

The story of the Widow of Nain is found in Luke 7:11–17.

My son, my precious son, is dead. I am a widow and my son is dead. What would happen to me now? I had no husband, no son and no male family members to provide for me. They might as well have been taking me out of the city to bury. As we were on our way to bury my son, a large crowd approached us. The man who seemed to be the leader moved toward me and told me not to cry. He seemed to have great compassion for me and understand my situation. The most miraculous thing happened! The man touched the bier on which my son's body lay and told my son to rise. He did! My son came back to life at the command of this compassionate man. Who is this man who has authority over life and death?

Words cannot describe my joy and fear. Our Scriptures tell of the great prophet Elijah, who restored life to the widow's son. Because of that deed, the widow recognized Elijah as a great man of God, a

---

6 Newsom and Ringe, 269.

man of truth. Now I, a widow, least among the people, had my son restored to me. Many of the people who witnessed my son's return from the dead proclaimed this man a prophet like Elijah, and word began to spread about him.

The Crippled Woman Tells Her Story

The story of the Crippled Woman is found in Luke 13:10–17.

He was in the synagogue. I knew he must be there because of the crowd. I was accustomed to being shunned by the people, but he spoke to me, a crippled old woman. I could not see his face because I had not been able to stand straight for eighteen years, but I could hear the kindness in his voice, not the way most people spoke to me. He called me "woman" an expression of great respect. I was trembling. Then he touched my shoulders and I could feel myself changing. I was able to stand up straight. After eighteen years, the first face I saw was this man smiling at me. Oh, what a precious gift from God this man was! There were no words to express my gratitude, though I tried. I praised him, and I praised God for this miracle in my life. There were many in the synagogue who praised God and rejoiced with me but the leaders of the synagogue were indignant that he had healed me, on the Sabbath. They yelled at the people to go away and come back another day. But this man put the well-being of people above the law. He called the leaders "Hypocrites!" They acted as if they were ashamed of themselves, but I did not believe it. I feared for the safety of this remarkable man.

The Poor Widow Tells Her Story

The Poor Widow is found in both Mark 12:41–44 and Luke 21:1–4.

I had nothing but two copper coins. They were not worth much to anyone but me. He was watching me as I put them in the treasury. I thought it was strange that he lingered in the Court of the Women. I heard him tell the people standing around that I had put in more than all of them because I had given out of the little I had. I felt proud that someone recognized my sacrifice.

Observations on the Widow of Nain, the Crippled Woman and the Poor Widow

These three women form a core of the compassionate work of Jesus. They have not asked Jesus for help. Jesus sees their need and comes to their rescue. In reference to the Crippled Woman, *The New Oxford Annotated Bible* explains, "Such afflictions conflict with God's purpose of salvation in God's covenant with Abraham and are the concerns of Jesus' ministry." (NRSV) In Luke 4:18–21, Jesus is reported to have read from the scroll of Isaiah. To paraphrase the words of the prophet, the Spirit of the Lord is upon me because I have been anointed to bring good news to the poor. I have been sent to proclaim release to those held in captivity, to restore sight to the blind, to give liberty to the oppressed and to proclaim the year of the Lord.

The widow of Nain was on her way to bury her son and, in so doing, would lose her status and possibly her livelihood. There is every indication that the widow of Nain was old because her son is referred to as a man. A widowed woman could return to her father's house or marry her brother-in-law, but an old woman would have no father's house to return to. Women had inferior economic status. With no husband or son to provide for her, she was effectively destitute. Psalms 146:9 states, among other things, that the Lord watches over and upholds widows. Jesus is demonstrating God's special option for the widow "fulfilling the Psalms, the Law and the Prophets."[8] Jesus had compassion for her because of her grief. But his compassion extended beyond her grief. In the male-dominated society in which they lived, without a male family member to care for her, she

[7] Nancy Corran, written message to author, July 2011.

would be financially helpless, with no one to speak on her behalf in a court of law. Jesus' mission was to release the captive and oppressed wherever he found them.

Jesus had compassion for the crippled woman. He healed her on the Sabbath. Jesus performed many healings on the Sabbath. Peter's mother-in-law was healed on the Sabbath. A man with dropsy was healed on the Sabbath in Luke 14:1–6. A demon-possessed man was healed on the Sabbath in Luke 4:31–37. A man with a withered hand was healed on the Sabbath in Luke 6:6–11. The commentary in *The New Oxford Annotated Bible,* for the healing of the man with dropsy, states, "The healing story forms the second part of a balanced pair with the foregoing account of Jesus: healing the crippled woman, exhibiting Luke's concern to show the inclusive nature of Jesus' ministry." (NRSV) These healings on the Sabbath demonstrate Jesus' concern for people above social constructs and religious regulations. His compassion is not constrained by gender. All are worthy of human dignity before God.

Is Jesus praising the widow who has just put all she had in the treasury, or is he mourning her poverty? In the preceding verses, Jesus is speaking to his disciples so that all the people can hear. Jesus says to beware of the scribes who, among other things, like to be greeted with respect, have the best seats in the synagogue and at banquets, and who devour widows' houses. I believe Jesus is mourning her poverty. If, as Psalm 146:9 states, the Lord watches over and upholds the widow, then the poor widow should not be taking care of the temple; the temple should be taking care of the poor widow.

Women in the Parables of Jesus

Jesus taught in parables. Matthew 13:34 states, "Jesus told the crowds all these things in parables; without a parable he told them nothing." (NRSV) In four of those parables, women are the main characters. I do not believe Jesus' intention in his parables was to offer concise sayings to make his listeners feel good. Jesus' intention was to shake up his listeners and shatter the status quo. He and his parables cut to the heart of the injustices of the social and religious establishments of his time.

The New International Dictionary of the Bible states that a parable is "a comparison of two objects for the purpose of teaching."[9] William Herzog, in *Parables as Subversive Speech,* says the basic meaning of parable is "riddle."[10] Ezekiel 17:2 states that God wants Ezekiel to speak a riddle to the people. In Matthew 13:10, the disciples ask Jesus why he teaches in parables. Jesus answers that, among other reasons, he speaks in parables because "seeing they do not perceive, and hearing they do not listen, nor do they understand." In Matthew 13:36 even the friends of Jesus need Jesus to explain the meaning of the parable to them and in Mark 4:13 Jesus chides them: "Do you not understand this parable?" (NAB) The authentic parables of Jesus were not easy or simple. They were difficult and thought provoking.

In an insightful note written in the margin of this manuscript, my friend and reader Hilary wrote, "If a person listens to a teacher, it is passive learning. If a person solves a riddle, it is active learning. Maybe Jesus is empowering people through his parables. They are more apt to accept his teachings because they participated in the process."[11]

The Parable of the Baking Woman is Found in Matthew 13:33 and Luke 13:20–21

Jesus said, "What is the reign of God like? It is like the yeast that a woman puts in three measures of flour until it is all leavened."

We read the parables through the lens of interpretation: first, the interpretation of the gospel writers and then of the men who have interpreted the Scriptures ever since. One of the first women to teach theology in the United States and thus produce theological

---

8 *The New International Dictionary of the Bible* (1987), s.v. "Parable."

9 William R. Herzog II, *Parables as Subversive Speech: Jesus as Pedagogue of the Oppressed* (Louisville: Westminster/John Knox Press, 1994), 11.

10 Hilary Christiansen, written message to author, July 2011.

interpretations for public consumption was Georgia Harkness in the mid 1920s. How would the people hearing the parables of Jesus understand them? Would they be surprised to hear the domestic chores of a woman compared to the reign of God? In the parable of the baking woman above, Jesus compares the reign of God in the world to a small amount of yeast which a woman mixes in three measures of flour. That was the same amount of flour that Abraham asked Sarah, in Genesis 18:6, to use in making cakes for the heavenly visitors. According to *The Women's Bible Commentary,* "This was approximately a bushel and was thus the largest amount of dough a person could knead. The bread produced could feed about one hundred people. Here work traditionally associated with women is recognized as having value. The final point is that the message of the *basilea* ("realm"), although hidden like a small bit of leaven in a mound of dough, will become—through this woman's effort—the bread of life."[12]

My nephew once asked me, "Why is it that women cook but all the best chefs are men?" This was at a time before the Food Network and, with the exception of Julia Child, the only chefs seen on television were men. My answer to him was, "Work women do in the home is not truly valued by most societies, but the work men do in public is." The *New Webster's Dictionary of the English Language*, published in 1971, defines a chef as "A male head cook who is in charge of a kitchen."[13] In this parable, Jesus legitimizes the value of women's work—work conducted in the private sphere of women as opposed to the public sphere of men. Jesus equates this woman's work with the action of God in the world. William Herzog calls it a parable of growth "which declares the arrival of the kingdom as a small and seemingly insignificant presence in the world that will, in time, grow to full stature."[14]

---

11 Newsom and Ringe, 258.

12 *New Webster's Dictionary of the English Language* (1981) s.v. "chef."

13 Herzog, 10.

The Parable of the Ten Bridesmaids is found in Matthew 25:1–13

Jesus said, "The realm of heaven will be like ten bridesmaids who took their lamps and went out to meet the groom. As they were waiting, five of the lamps burned out, and the girls ran off to buy more oil. The groom arrived while the girls were away. The rest of the wedding party went in, and the door was shut. When the girls returned they could not get in."

The actions of the bridesmaids is employed here to demonstrate preparedness for the reign of God. There is, however, some question about whether this parable is an authentic parable of Jesus. "The story does not have any of the earmarks of Jesus' authentic parables. It does not cut against the religious and social grain. Rather, it confirms common wisdom: those who are prepared will succeed, those not prepared will fail."[15] The parable is included here because, although it may not be an authentic parable of Jesus, it does highlight the actions of women.

The Parable of the Woman and the Lost Coin is found in Luke 15:8–10

Jesus said, "What woman who has lost one of her ten coins will not light the lamp and sweep her house until she finds it? In her joy she invites her neighbors to rejoice with her. You are more precious to God than the coin is to that poor women."

Luke reports that while Jesus is telling this parable, the scribes and Pharisees are grumbling about Jesus' choice of dinner companions: tax collectors and sinners. The woman in this parable has lost a coin, one of only ten that she has. She is depicted as sweeping, an activity thought of as woman's work, to retrieve the coin. Her ten coins were equivalent to ten days' wages for a day laborer, a minimum-wage job. Those listening to the parable would have understood that this

---

14 Robert Funk and Roy W. Hoover, *The Five Gospels: The Search for the Authentic Words of Jesus* (New York: Macmillan Publishing Company, 1993), 254.

was a poor woman and that the ten coins were possibly all that stood between her and starvation.

When she finds the coin, she is overjoyed and probably very relieved. She invites her friends to celebrate with her, because she has found her day's wage. According to the website of the United States Department of Labor, the federal minimum wage, as of November 13, 2013, was $7.25 per hour. In modern terms, her coin would be equivalent to fifty-eight dollars, a day's wage for a minimum-wage earner before taxes. For the poor and the working poor, this is a great deal of money.

During the time I was contemplating this parable, I went Christmas shopping. When I got home with my packages, I discovered that some of the items I had paid for had not been put into my bags. I was heartsick. Although I am not among those who work for minimum wage, I had a sense of what the woman in the parable must have felt, losing a whole day's wages. As in the parable of the leaven in bread, "The woman sweeping and seeking the coin is freely cast in the parable to depict the activity of God." (NRSV) God's love for the lost is demonstrated by the woman in the parable.

The Parable of the Justified Widow is found in Luke 18:2–4

Jesus said, "There was a poor widow in a town where a very corrupt judge presided. The widow begged him for justice time and time again. Finally, the judge granted her request. Not because he was a good and honest judge, but because the widow was bothering him. Call on God for justice, and God will not be slow to answer."

This parable is sometimes called the "Unjust Judge" or the "Persistent Widow." Luke's introduction to the parable has Jesus saying that the parable is an encouragement to pray and not lose heart. William R. Herzog offers a much more tantalizing interpretation. Herzog focuses on how the hearers of Jesus' parables would have understood Jesus.

Remember that Luke was not an eyewitness to Jesus, as he declares in Luke 1:1–4. So when he says that Jesus told the parable to encourage his listeners to pray and not lose heart, Luke is expressing his own interpretation of Jesus' intention for the parable.

The widow is a poor and helpless woman. "A number of scholars have suggested that the very presence of a widow at court is in itself an extraordinary event that witnesses to her vulnerability. Women did not normally appear at court but were represented by a male family member. Indeed, the very fact that the widow in the parable has appeared before the judge is a breach of etiquette. That she is representing herself may indicate that she has no family to which she can appeal for help. In this condition, her life may depend on the settlement of her case."[16] Like the gentile woman who approaches Jesus for help with her sick daughter, the poor widow has stepped out of her expected silence to get help. Like Tamar, she is taking control of her life and her situation.

The Hebrew Scriptures are brimming with examples of God's special care for widows, orphans and strangers living among the people. Deuteronomy 27:19 says, "Cursed be anyone who deprives the alien (stranger), the orphan and the widow of justice." (NRSV) The judge in the parable is often interpreted as a symbol for God. Jesus is quoted as saying, "Will not God grant justice to his chosen ones who cry to him day and night?" (NRSV) As Herzog makes clear, Jesus uses the parable to illustrate how those in covenant with God are supposed to act toward each other and contrasts that with the reality of what is happening in the lives of poor and widowed women, the very individuals the law is supposed to protect. "The widow refuses to quit and threatens to blow the cover off the whole system. Her reward is justice at the gate."[17]

---

[15] Herzog, 228.

[16] Herzog, 231.

Prostitutes

In Matthew 21:31, Jesus tells the chief priests and elders that prostitutes and tax collectors will enter the realm of God before the chief priests and elders. Levi, a tax collector, was a member of the inner circle who traveled with Jesus. It is altogether possible that there were prostitutes who traveled with Jesus as well. It is to the chief priests and elders, the religious leaders, that Jesus addresses these words. What can we imagine Jesus meant by this saying? What was Jesus' understanding of the hardship of the lives of these women? "Prostitution evolves out of the profound social and economic problems confronting adolescent females."[18] Research conducted by R. Tong and reported in *Women, Law and Social Control* states, "A majority of prostitutes (65 percent) were raped as children."[19] Granted, it is anachronistic to apply twenty-first-century statistics to first-century women. However, women who are economically, physically, educationally and socially secure rarely choose a life in which they will be economically, physically and sexually abused. The world in which Jesus lived was bursting with injustice and oppression. Our world is bursting with injustice and oppression. Jesus recognized and spoke out against injustice and oppression. The religious leaders must have been highly insulted to hear Jesus praise prostitutes, who, like prostitutes today, are reviled by religious society. Jesus makes it clear that the offenses of the religious leaders are greater than those of these women. Remember, in Mark 12:38, Jesus warns those listening to beware of the religious leaders because, among other things, they like to walk around in long robes, be greeted with respect, have the seat of honor and devour the homes of widows.

Conclusion

If you have ever played the child's game of "telephone," you know that, by the time the message gets around the room, it bears little

---

[17] Katherine Stuart van Wormer and Clemens Bartollas, *Women and the Criminal Justice System* (New York: Pearson Education Inc., 2007), 79.

[18] Merlo and Pollock, 26.

resemblance to what was originally whispered. The message changes as it is passed on from one person to the next. As noted above, the book of Mark was the first of our canonical gospels and was not written until 30 to 40 years after the crucifixion. During that time, the "stories" of Jesus' life and works were circulated orally and in written form. Just as the message whispered in the game of "telephone" is changed as it passes from one person to another, so the stories of Jesus changed as they were repeated, eventually written, copied, and recopied. The stories also changed based on the context in which they were told and the agenda of the messenger.

Jesus demonstrated over and over again his concern for equal treatment of people. He treated the Samaritan woman at Jacob's well as an equal in his conversation with her. He accepted the touch of the ritually unclean hemorrhaging woman. He shared meals with tax collectors and others viewed as ritually unclean. Women were the faithful disciples at the crucifixion, the burial and at the tomb.

The layers of patriarchal interpretation get encrusted so thickly that we do not even know why we believe what we believe. We believe what the interpreters have told us to believe, beginning with the original writers of the gospels and epistles. They wrote from their own personal or communal understanding of the life, words and actions of Jesus. There is no independent woman's interpretation of her experience of the Divine in the entire Bible. God is not a respecter of people or institutions, men over women, whites over other ethnicities, the United States over other nations, rich over poor. The mission of Jesus was, as ours should be today, to change structures of injustice and oppression.

Jesus treated women as equals. The argument against women teaching men in the church is often repeated in some circles. It was, however, the unnamed gentile woman who taught Jesus that his mission was to the world and not just to the lost sheep of Israel. Jesus was not afraid of the lesson taught by this woman. He praised her for her faith and granted her request for the healing of her daughter. It was the Samaritan woman at the well who "evangelized" her entire village. Men and women alike came to faith in Jesus because of her teaching. She had to teach the village about Jesus; she was the one Jesus had chosen. It was to this woman that Jesus revealed himself as the Messiah. It was the women followers of Jesus who were the first to proclaim the resurrection to the unbelieving male disciples. They had to tell the male disciples about the resurrection. They were commissioned by angels and by Jesus himself. It is obvious, from the biblical text, that women were among those Jesus taught about the resurrection. As stated above, in Mark 16:7, a young man tells the women that they will see Jesus "just as he told you." (NRSV) In Matthew 28:6, an angel tells the women, "He has been raised, as he said." (NRSV) And in Luke 24:6, it is two men who remind the women, "Remember how he told you, while he was still in Galilee, that the Son of Man must be handed over to sinners, and be crucified, and on the third day rise again." (NRSV) In all three incidences the women are reminded of what Jesus has taught them. Women were with Jesus, traveling with him, ministering to him, learning from him and being commissioned by him. That some later Christian writers and the men who decided what our biblical canon should be did not include the women or call them "disciples" and "apostles" should not stop us from granting these women their rightful place in the community of Jesus.

Chapter Seven

WOMEN IN THE DEVELOPMENT OF THE EARLY CHURCH AND IN THE EPISTLES

What happened to all the women who were the family and friends of Jesus? Mary, his mother, is mentioned in the book of Acts along with the other women who received the Holy Spirit on Pentecost. The wife of Peter is mentioned only once, in First Corinthians, although her name is not recorded. As the community was growing, what were the roles of the women who had been eyewitnesses and friends of Jesus? What about his sisters or Mary Magdalene or Peter's mother-in-law and Peter's wife or Salome, one or both of the disciples on the road to Emmaus, Martha and her sister Mary? There is a long list of the women who knew Jesus in his life, but they are never mentioned again in the Bible. Their stories were not recorded.

Why did all those other women disappear? I think the answer is that the work men do outside the home is honored more than the work women do inside the home. The early church grew in the homes of women and men. "Much of what women do is undervalued because many men see the work as reflecting innate gender characteristics. What women do inside and outside the home is often labeled as 'women's work' and thus as not terribly important. Men are responsible for property; women for persons. The latter are evaluated as less important and less skilled than the former."[1]

Who were the women in the first century church? Was Paul's sister a member of the early church? She is mentioned in Acts 23:12–22. Women were instrumental leaders in the early church. It was not until the church started to go public, so to speak, that the leadership roles of women, in fact, the very humanity of women, came into question. Because of the patriarchal, hierarchical structure of most churches today, the importance of women in the early church and the roles they played have been forgotten, ignored or rationalized away. When Pentecost is celebrated on Pentecost Sunday, it is often the verses in Acts 2:1–15 which are taught—verses which proclaim the arrival of the Holy Spirit with rushing winds, tongues of fire and individuals speaking foreign languages. Verse 1:14 is often ignored. This verse explains that the women and the mother of Jesus were part of that group. Also often ignored is Acts 2:17, in which God is quoted as saying that an equal portion of God's Spirit will be poured out, on all and sons, daughters, servants and handmaids will prophesy.

In Acts and the Epistles, women are called disciples, prophets, co-workers, deacons, church leaders, apostles and saints. And yet, in the interest of limiting women's full participation in the church, what we are taught about women in the New Testament are those verses which try to limit a woman's participation in the church. We know women were praying and prophesying in the early church. First Corinthians

1 Nijole V. Benokraitis and Joe R. Feagin, *Modern Sexism: Blatant, Subtle, and Covert Discrimination* (Englewood Cliffs: Prentice Hall, 1986), 101.

11:5 instructs women to pray or prophesy with their heads covered. It does not tell women *not* to pray and prophesy in church.

Where to Find the Story of the Prophetic Daughters of Philip

Four of those prophesying women are found in the Acts of the Apostles. They are the daughters of Philip, one of the seven men appointed to serve or minister to the widows. All we know from the Bible about these four prophesying women is that Philip "had four unmarried daughters who had the gift of prophecy." (NRSV) Happily, later historians record the importance of these women to the early church. The biblical story of their father appears in Acts 6:1–5; 8:5–7; 8:12; 8:26–40 and 21:8–14. As unmarried women, they most likely lived with their father. If that is so, they were probably witnesses to the events recorded in the life of their father Philip.

The Prophesying Daughters of Philip Tell Their Story

We were there when our father was appointed one of the seven who were to minister to the widows. We were also there when Stephen, another of the seven, was stoned to death. It was about that time the persecution against the church began in Jerusalem. Many of us fled. First, we traveled in Samaria. Our father, much like Jesus, was fond of disregarding religious and social obstacles. He told the Samaritans about Jesus and baptized as many women and men as believed. One community remembered the woman of Samaria, who was the first to teach them about Jesus.

We were there when our father disregarded yet another religious barrier and baptized the Ethiopian eunuch. Our Scriptures say that if a man's testicles are crushed or if his penis is cut off, he shall not be admitted to the assembly of the Lord. But our father remembered the inclusive nature of Jesus' teaching.

We found ourselves in Azotus and eventually settled in a beautiful seacoast town in Samaria called Caesarea. Our father was a wise man, and we, his daughters, had been given the gift of prophecy by the Holy Spirit. We were there when Paul showed up. He had long since stopped persecuting the church and had become one of us. Agabus and others urged him not to go to Jerusalem but, no one could talk him out of it.

Observations on the Prophesying Daughters of Philip

"Prophets and teachers were important leaders in the early church." (NRSV) Acts 21:9 records that Philip had four daughters "which did prophesy." *The New Oxford Annotated* says the young women "had the gift of prophecy." (NRSV) Unfortunately, the names and prophecies of these women are not recorded in the Bible. Instead, the prophecy of Agabus is recorded.

Miriam Therese Winter writes that the sisters "are acknowledged by Eusebius the historian as women prophets and transmitters of apostolic tradition whose fame was great in Asia."[2] The Eusebius to whom she refers was a church historian and the bishop of the church in Caesarea, the city in which the daughters of Philip lived. He wrote between 263 and 339 C.E. *The New Oxford Annotated Bible* says, "Philip's daughters became important figures in the church tradition of Hierapolis and Ephesus." (NRSV)

Polycrates, the bishop of Ephesus, wrote between 185 and 195 C.E. In a letter concerning the observance of Passover, he says of the sisters, "For in Asia great luminaries have gone to their rest, who shall rise again in the day of the coming of the Lord, when he cometh with glory from heaven and shall rise again all the saints. I speak of Philip, one of the twelve apostles who is laid to rest at Hierapolis, and his two daughters who arrived at old age unmarried, his other daughter also, who passed her life under the influence of the

[2] Winter, *Woman Word*, 218.

Holy Spirit and repose at Ephesus.[3] In this list of luminaries, which included the prophetic daughters of Philip, Polycrates includes the disciple who "reclined on the Lord's bosom." Although Polycrates calls Philip one of the twelve, he was one of the seven who served the widows.

Other writings attest to the importance of the prophetic sisters. The writings of Papias, bishop of Hierapolis, have not survived. "Eusebius speaks of Papias' stories of the daughters of Philip."[4] Likewise, Miltiades, a pope who died in 314 C.E., cited the women in his writing. The book of Acts begins on the day of Pentecost with Peter quoting the prophet Joel, "In the last days it will be, God declares that I will pour out my spirit upon all flesh, and your sons and your daughters shall prophesy." (NRSV) Does it make sense that God would give women the gift of prophecy and not want them to use that gift in the church?

There are many more female prophets in both Hebrew and Christian Scripture. Some are called prophets, and others demonstrate prophetic ability. Miriam, the sister of Moses, is called a prophet in Exodus 15:20. Judges 4:4 declares Deborah a prophet and a judge to whom the Israelites came for judgment. These roles were traditionally reserved for a man. She also summons Barak to lead a war against the Canaanites, explains the strategy to him and accompanies him into battle. When he refuses to go without her, she prophesies that God will deliver their enemy into the hands of a woman and the glory shall not belong to him. Huldah is named a prophet twice: first in Second Kings 22:14 and then in Second Chronicles 34:22. Noadiah is remembered as a prophet who wanted to make Nehemiah afraid in Nehemiah 6:14. Isaiah, the prophet, is married to a prophet in Isaiah

---

3 Peter Kirby, "Polycrates Bishop of Ephesus," *Early Christian Writings*. February 2, 2006. http://www.earlychristianwritings.com/text/polycrates.html.

4 Rob Bradshaw, "Papias (Early Second Century)," *Theology on the Web*. February 16, 2011. http://www.earlychurch.org.uk/papias.php.

8:3. Anna, the prophet in Luke 2:36, has already been remembered among the women in the public life of Jesus.

Rahab, one of the women in Jesus' genealogy, demonstrates prophetic ability in her conversation with the spies sent by Joshua. In Joshua 2:9 she says to them, "I know that the Lord has given you the land, and that dread of you has fallen on us, and that all the inhabitants of the land melt in fear before you." (NRSV) At that point in the narration of the story, Joshua's people did not yet possess the land.

Both Mary and Elizabeth prophesy in the first verse of Luke. Elizabeth asks, "Why has this happened to me, that the mother of my Lord comes to me?" (NRSV) This was before the birth of Mary's son. Mary announces, "From now on all generations will call me blessed." (NRSV) Finally, the wife of Pilate, in Matthew 27:19, begs her husband to have nothing to do with the innocent Jesus because of a dream she had about him.

Where to Find the Story of Tabatha the Disciple

Who were the women who came to faith in Jesus after the resurrection? The book of Acts and the Epistles name many of them. Tabatha, featured next, is described as a disciple. Her story is found in Acts 9:36–42.

Tabatha Tells Her Story

I am a disciple living in Joppa. I work in the church, support it financially and minister to widows and others. I understand how important service to the widows is. In Jerusalem, seven men were commissioned to serve the widows in their church. Our Scriptures declare that God puts great importance on the care of widows. In Deuteronomy 10:17–19, God says, "For the Lord your God is God of gods and Lord of lords, the great God mighty and awesome, who is not partial and takes no bribe, who executes justice for the orphan and the widow, and who loves the strangers, providing them food and clothing." (NRSV) This was my work. Jesus condemned some of the religious leaders for their treatment of widows, and he praised a poor widow for her meager contribution to the temple treasury.

I got sick and, as the other disciples tell it, I died. I don't remember anything, but when I woke up, Peter was with me. I was so surprised to see him that I sat right up. He offered his hand to help me. He had learned from Jesus not to treat women, the sick or the ritually unclean any differently from healthy, free men. There was great rejoicing among the disciples when Peter brought me to them. My story spread quickly, and many women and men were added to our number. When Peter left us, he went to stay with Simon the Tanner. As a tanner, Simon was one of those considered ritually unclean. Peter was becoming more like Jesus every day.

Observations on Tabatha

The name Tabatha is Greek. In Aramaic, the language Jesus probably spoke, her name is Dorcas. Joppa is a seacoast town about thirty-five miles north of Jerusalem. Tabatha must have been an important person in the church in Joppa. She is called a disciple. Her function was to serve or minister to the widows, as Philip, Stephen and the other five men do in Acts 6:5, yet her commissioning is not recorded.

There was great urgency on the part of the members of the church to help Tabatha. Two men went to Lydda to fetch Peter. On his arrival, he raised her from the dead, in much the same way Jesus raised the daughter of Jairus in the gospels.

All too often, we are taught only about the men who are said to accompany Jesus in his public work. However, here is a woman, recognized as a disciple, who is not reported in the public life of Jesus. The women who ministered to Jesus were disciples. The seven men commissioned to serve the widows were disciples. Women were not to be denied discipleship simply because of their gender. Tabatha is an example from Scripture of a woman who was a disciple.

Where to Find the Story of Rhoda and Mary, the Mother of John Mark

The stories of the next two women are linked together. Rhoda is a servant in the home of Mary, the mother of John Mark. After the murder of James, one of the male disciples of Jesus, the members of the church who met in Mary's home are together, praying for Peter who has been arrested. Their story is found in Acts 12:11–17.

Rhoda Tells Her Story

I am employed in the home of Mary, the mother of John Mark. Mary leads a church in our home. I say "our" home, but Mary, of course, owns the house. She has always treated me as a family member. One night we were all together, praying for Peter. He had been thrown in prison. Herod had killed James, one of Salome's sons. We were all terribly sad.

As I was going about my duties, I heard knocking on the outer gate of the courtyard. Peter had been in our home many times, and I immediately recognized his voice. In my excitement, I ran to tell the assembly that Peter was at the gate. They told me I was crazy and that it was his angel. We were all so worried! What if Peter suffered the same fate as James?

I ran back to the gate and let him in. He was very patient with my enthusiasm. He had no harsh words for me. I could not believe I had left him at the gate. They should have all been very cross with me, but ours is a community based on the example of Jesus. We did not rank members of our community based on education, occupation, age or gender. In our community we are all equals, and we each use our special gifts to help the community.

Everyone was amazed and delighted to see him. Peter told us what he had been through and left us with instructions to tell James, the brother of Jesus, what had happened. I am sure he was trying to protect our community in case Herod's soldiers came looking for him. He also needed to put as much distance between himself and Herod as possible.

Observations on Rhoda's Story

Rhoda's story is the situation comedy of biblical literature. A servant girl leaves the male protagonist knocking at the gate instead of letting him in! Peter had just been through the terrible ordeal of escaping from prison. Rhoda has recognized his voice and run off to tell the household that he is at the gate. The male protagonist continues to knock while the maid is away and, of course, the people Rhoda has gone to tell do not believe her and even tell her she is out of her mind. She was probably a member of the community that prayed together in Mary's home.

Except for the disbelief of the others, there is no pejorative statement about her actions. She is not criticized for allowing Peter to stand knocking at the gate, as one might expect in a hierarchical household. She had spent enough time in the company of Peter to recognize his voice from the other side of the gate. She also appears to have great affection for Peter. *The New Oxford Annotated* says she was "overjoyed" (NRSV) to hear his voice.

Mary, the Mother of John Mark, Tells Her Story

That girl! Well, who can blame her? She is young, and we were all so fearful for Peter! We did not believe her when she told us he was at the gate. I'm sure she couldn't believe her own ears. She was right, though. Peter *was* at the gate. It could have been dangerous for him to be left standing out there! What if he had been followed? It could have been dangerous for all of us. We were so very sad about the murder of James and so ecstatic to see Peter alive. He told us the miracle of his escape and that he had come directly to us. He did not stay with us; I think he was afraid he would put the church in my home in danger.

Observations on Mary's Story

Mary appears to be a wealthy and independent woman. She is referred to as the mother of John Mark, not as the wife of someone. As a widow, she may have inherited her property. She has at least one servant and a home large enough to hold an assembly of people. The home is separated from the street by a courtyard with a gate. The text says that Peter went directly to Mary's house when he escaped from prison. It does not say that Peter went to John Mark's house. "Wherever Christianity spread, women were leaders of house churches. Mary, the mother of John Mark, presided over a house church of Hellenistic Jews in Jerusalem."[5] The text does not tell us who the members of the community were. However, we can speculate that the communities which grew up around the teachings of Jesus and the examples of his life consisted of both women and men. One congregation, however, appears to be made up exclusively of women in the town of Philippi.

Where to Find the Story of Lydia

The next biblical woman, Lydia, had a community of believers in her home after her baptism. She also appears to have been a member of a community of women who met for prayer. She was a resident of the town of Philippi. There is a gap in her story. Her house guests, Paul and his companions, get thrown into prison between the time she invites them to stay with her and the time they depart for Thessalonica. Paul's letter to the Philippians may have been written to the church in Lydia's home. Her story is recorded in Acts 16:11–40. In verses 4:1–4 of his letter to the Philippians, Paul exhorts two women, Euodia and Syntyche, who have labored with him, to agree on an unknown topic. These women may have been members of the church in Lydia's home.

Lydia Tells Her Story

I sell purple cloth in the Roman colony of Philippi. As such, I am a wealthy, respected businesswoman. I worship with a group of women who gather by the river on Sabbath mornings to pray. One morning, some men joined us. One of them, named Paul, told us about a man

[5] Karen Torjensen, *When Women Were Priests: Women's Leadership in the Early Church & the Scandal of their Subordination in the Rise of Christianity* (San Francisco: Harper, 1995), 33.

named Jesus. Jesus stood against injustice, spoke to women openly as these men were doing, and epitomized the God of the Jews, the God I had been praying to with the other women. What these men said thrilled my heart. I asked to be baptized and, as head of my household, my household was baptized with me.

I invited the men to stay in my home. They ran into trouble with some of the people in the town, and I was helpless to do anything for them. When they were finally released from prison, they came back to stay with me before continuing on their journey. The church that grew in my home sent assistance to Paul and his companions. He wrote loving letters to us. He was very concerned when our sisters, Syntyche and Euodia, had their now-famous disagreement. He commended them for the work they had done alongside Clement, himself and the others. He begged us to help them resolve their conflict, which we did.

Observations on the Story of Lydia, Euodia and Syntyche

Lydia, Euodia and Syntyche lived in Philippi. Lydia is mentioned in the Book of Acts as being at a gathering of women who pray together. Paul and his companions encounter the women at prayer outside the city gates. We know nothing about Euodia and Syntyche except that they are mentioned in Paul's letter to the Philippians. They are women who labored with Paul and others in the work of the gospel. They also have some kind of a disagreement that is a concern for Paul.

A community of believers met in Lydia's home. It is to this community that Paul and his companions, who have been in prison, return. Perhaps Lydia, Euodia and Syntyche were members of the same community, working together to spread the good news of Jesus. Lydia's entire household was baptized with her. "Dependents followed the head of the household in religious matters." (NRSV) Paul praises Euodia and Syntyche in the same sentence in which he praises Clement for the work they have done. There appears to be no difference in the commendation of the two women and the man.

This fact is often overlooked because of the disagreement the two women are having. Was the work these women were doing with Paul, Clement and others preaching, teaching and baptizing? Paul says they proclaimed the gospel. Whatever their work was, Paul seems to place great value on it and on the women. He also shows great concern that their disagreement be resolved for the good of the church in Philippi.

Where to Find the Story of Women in the Church in Rome

In the concluding chapter of the book of Romans 16:1–15, Paul cites ten women for recognition and praise. Phoebe is the first. She is called a "*diakonos,*" translated in *The King James* version of the *Bible* as "servant" and in *The New Oxford Annotated Bible,* published in 2010, as "deacon" or "minister" of the church in Cenchreae. "Worthy of note, at the time this was written, 'deacon' was already an official position in the church."[6] Another woman, Priscilla, also called Prisca, was cited. Priscilla is also found in the book of Acts, First Corinthians, and Second Timothy. The other women cited are Julia, Junia, Mary, Persis, Tryphaena, Tryphosa, the unnamed sister of Nereus, and the unnamed mother of Rufus. None of these women have a voice, and all we know about them is what Paul has to say about these "women of action."[7]

Phoebe Tells Her Story

I am the leader of the church in Cenchreae near Corinth. I was privileged to deliver Paul's letter to the church in Rome. What a joy to finally meet the saints in Rome: Priscilla, who had risked her life, not only for Paul but also as a teacher of the gospel; the apostle Junia, who had been in prison with Paul; and Paul's dear friend, the beloved Persis. We had heard of the work of Mary, Tryphaena and Tryphosa.

---

6 Nancy Corran, written message to author, July 2011.

7 *Ibid.*

When I met them, I understood why Paul was so impressed. I met Julia and the sister of Nereus. Finally, I met the mother of Rufus, who had been like a mother to Paul. They were very good to me. Paul had directed them to take care of me in whatever I needed. I don't think those instructions were necessary. They were such wonderful women.

Observations on Phoebe and the Other Women in the Book of Romans

Phoebe, in *The King James,* is called a sister and a servant of the church. "Paul's introduction of Phoebe as 'our sister and *diakonos*' parallels that of Timothy as 'our brother and God's *diakonos*' (First Thess, 3:2) and Tychicus as 'our beloved brother and faithful *diakonos*' (Col 4:7). Traditionally, the word, when used to describe men, has been translated 'minister' or 'missionary,' but when applied to Phoebe, a woman, it has been given a subsidiary meaning such as 'deaconess' or 'helper.'"[8]

In the gospels, the word *diakonos* is translated as "servant" in reference to the actions of Peter's mother-in-law and Martha of Bethany. In Ephesians 3:7, the word *diakonos* is translated as "minister" in reference to Paul, and First Corinthians 3:5 translates *diakonos* as "minister" when referring to Paul and Apollos. In Romans 15:8, *diakonos* is translated as "servant" in reference to Jesus in his mission to the Jewish community. The function of the seven men in Acts 6 is to serve widows. "These seven are identified as the first deacons by later tradition but hold no ecclesiastical office here." (NRSV)

Why has the same Greek word been translated differently when it refers to women than when it refers to men? What is the benefit of translating a word to imply that men are ministers or deacons but women are mere servants or helpers? The problem is that the interpretations of the translations are used to exclude women from their positions of leadership in the church. "Scripture reflects the bias of

8 Winter, *Woman Word*, 229.

the time it was written. The translations of Scripture reflect the bias of the translators."[9] If *diakonos* is translated as "servant" in reference to Jesus and women, that must equate the importance of the service performed by Jesus and by women. Likewise, if *diakonos* refers to the service of men, then their service is equivalent to that of Jesus and the women. There should not be a double standard that attempts to minimize what women were doing in the early church and increases the importance of what men did. Remember, in the gospels, it is only women and angels who minister to Jesus. If the word is to be translated as "minister" or "deacon," then it must be acknowledged that, from the earliest testimonies, there were women who served the function of deacons and ministers. There is ample biblical evidence that women were deacons, ministers, teachers, disciples and prophets in the early church.

Junia the Apostle

Junia, Paul declares, was in prison with him, was in Christ before him, and is prominent among the apostles. In First Corinthians 15:5–7, Paul says that the risen Christ appeared to, among others, Peter, the twelve, and then to all the apostles. The women at the empty tomb and the Samaritan woman at the well were all sent as messengers. "One of the Greek fathers of the church, John Chrysostom, not known for his affirmation of women, knew Junia was a woman and was amazed that she should be called an apostle."[10] The life of John Chrysostom is dated between 347 and 407 C.E. In this quote, taken from the website *Council on Biblical Manhood and Womanhood*, he states, "To be an apostle is something great. But to be outstanding among the apostles—just think what a wonderful song of praise that is! They were outstanding on the basis of their works and virtuous actions.

---

9 Nancy Corran, written message to author, July 2011.

10 Winter, *Woman Word*, 241.

Indeed, how great is the wisdom of this woman that she was even deemed worthy of the title."[11]

In Acts 13:2–3, the Holy Spirit requests that Saul (Paul) and Barnabas be set apart for the work to which they have been called. Later, in Acts 14:4, Paul and Barnabas are called "apostles." James, the brother of Jesus, is called an apostle in Galatians 1:19. We sometimes think that just the twelve men who travelled with Jesus were apostles. However there is ample evidence that more people were considered apostles than just the twelve, as First Corinthians, Acts and Galatians clearly demonstrate.

There is some disagreement about the translation of the name "Junia." *The King James Version* uses the name "Junia." Those who wish to deny that a woman could be an apostle want to translate the name as "Junias." "Junia was a common name in the ancient Roman world; Junias appears to have been completely unknown."[12] In light of this fact, it is argued that "Junias" is a contraction of a longer attested male name. As the authors of the book *Women in the Church: A Biblical Theology of Women in Ministry* point out, "as the use of Priscilla for Prisca illustrates, Latin names of endearment are normally lengthened forms, not shortened."[13]

Perhaps Andronicus and Junia formed a missionary team, as did Priscilla and Aquila. Church father Origen, writing two centuries before John Chrysostom, recognized "Junia" as a woman's name. "The earliest evidence of the shift to Junias, the male form, appears in the thirteenth-century writings of Aegidius of Rome."[14] Aegidius was a Scholastic philosopher and theologian who died in 1247 C.E. There are those who will go to any length to insist that a woman could not

---

[11] David Jones, "A Female Apostle?" *The Council on Biblical Manhood and Womanhood.* September 30, 2012. http://cbmw.org/uncategorized/a-female-apostle/.

[12] Grenz, 94.

[13] *Ibid.*

[14] Winter, *Woman Word*, 241.

have been an apostle, but early testimony and manuscripts from church fathers state that Junia, a woman, was an apostle.

We can only guess at the importance of the other women Paul greets in his letter to the Romans. The sister of Nereus, the mother of Rufus and Julia, are greeted with no elaboration except that Paul says the mother of Rufus was like a mother to him, also. Paul calls Mary, Persis, Tryphaena and Tryphosa women who have worked hard, either in the Lord or among the people. Additionally, he calls Persis "beloved." "The term Paul uses to refer to the 'working' of these women, *kopian,* is precisely the same verb he employs to describe his own apostolic labours (*cf.* e.g., First Cor. 15:10)."[15] As in his recommendation of Phoebe as a deacon and Junia as an apostle, Paul does not differentiate what he himself has done or what other men have done from the work women have done.

Where to Find the Story of Priscilla the Minister and Her Husband Aquila

This ministry team appears in Acts 18:1–3; 18:18; 18:24; First Corinthians 16:19; Romans 16:3; and Second Timothy 4:19.

Priscilla Tells Her Story

When we were ordered by Claudius to leave Rome with the rest of the Jews, I had no idea where we would go or what we would do. We journeyed toward Athens but stopped for a time in Corinth. While we were there, we met Paul. He was a tentmaker, as were we, so we lived together in Corinth.

When Paul resumed his journey, we travelled with him to Cenchreae. It was there that we met the deacon of the church, Phoebe. She was such great help and support to Paul and to us while we were there. We left Cenchreae and went as far as Ephesus with Paul. The

---

[15] Byrne, 73.

churches we left in Corinth and Cenchreae had many questions, and Paul wrote several letters to help them with their concerns.

When Paul was ready to leave Ephesus, we remained behind. We had established a church in our home there. It was good that we did. An articulate, enthusiastic man named Apollos visited us. He was well versed in Scripture but knew only the baptism of John. He needed further instruction. We took him in and taught him all we knew about Jesus.

The day I had long hoped for finally arrived. We got word that we could return to Rome. It was a long journey, but we proclaimed Jesus everywhere we went. It was so good to be home at last! We, of course, organized another church in our home. We were so happy to get a letter from our dear friend, Paul. He gave us the highest praise. He called us co-workers in Christ and acknowledged that we had risked our lives for him.

Observations on Priscilla

Priscilla, also called Prisca, is mentioned three times in the Book of Acts and in three of the epistles. Four of the six times she is cited with others, but her name is first. She, along with her husband, shared equally in tent making, establishing churches, taking risks, teaching and working with Paul. Paul commends them equally.

In his book, *The Apostle Paul and Women in the Church,* Don Williams states, "Nowhere is it suggested that Prisca is inferior to or under the authority of Aquila in ministry. To the contrary, she shares a title and task of equality as a 'fellow-worker.' She is a fellow-worker in suffering and in church building and is universally recognized as such."[16] I wish this were true. However, there are those who try to develop an argument against the public ministry or teaching of women.

[16] Don Williams, *The Apostle Paul & Women in the Church* (Ventura: Regal Books, a Division of G/L Publications, 1977), 43.

The Greek word *ektithemi,* translated as "explained" in both Acts 18:26 and 28:23, is used to depict both Priscilla's teaching of Apollos' and Paul's teaching of the Judean men in Rome. The argument is that Priscilla's teaching was in private, and Paul's teaching was in public. However, Paul was under house arrest in Acts 28:23. The text says the men went to Paul at his lodgings. Acts 28:16 says Paul was allowed to live by himself, with soldiers guarding him. Why do we believe what we believe? Understanding what is true demands biblical literacy. Priscilla and Paul taught in private and in public, although Priscilla's public teaching has not been recorded. The work women do, or have historically done, is in private and thus not recognized as valuable. Priscilla's teaching in a private setting is no less important than Paul's teaching in a private setting. Both were explaining the realm of God to their listeners. Apollos might have remained ignorant of the Gospel of Jesus if Priscilla had not been there to instruct him.

Erasing Women from the Bible

During my years teaching kindergarten, I experienced many encounters with male fear of being taught by a female. It is remarkable that, at such a young age, the boys have already accepted a patriarchal world view. In one such instance, I asked a little girl to show a little boy where the office was. "Wait a minute," another little boy shouted. "Girls can't teach boys how to do stuff." My response was, "Girls can if they already know the stuff."

Women had churches in their homes. Mary, the mother of John Mark, and Lydia have already been discussed. In both cases, there is no mention of a male head of household. The fact that Lydia's entire household was baptized with her indicates that she was, indeed, the head of her household. Priscilla had a church in the home she shared with Aquila. Priscilla, like Mary and Lydia, were the leaders of the churches in their homes.

Nympha, a woman who lived in Colossae, is greeted by Paul at the close of his letter to the Colossians. As in the case of Junia, whose name was mistranslated to reflect a male apostle instead of a female apostle, the name Nympha has been translated to reflect a man having a church in his home instead of a woman. *The New Oxford Annotated* translates the greeting sent to Nympha as "Give my greetings to the brothers and sisters in Laodicea, and to Nympha and the church in her house." (NRSV)

Apphia is greeted in Paul's letter to Philemon as a sister and is said to have a church in her home. In First Corinthians, it is "Chloe's people" who have informed Paul of the problems in the church in Corinth. Perhaps Chloe has a church in her home. Paul is familiar enough with Chloe to believe and be concerned by the reports of "her people."

Perhaps the mother and grandmother of Timothy have a church in their home. Second Timothy 1:5 says of them, "I am reminded of your sincere faith, a faith that lived first in your grandmother Lois and your mother Eunice and now, I am sure, lives in you." (NRSV)

The identity of the Elect Lady and her children, to whom the second letter of John is addressed, mirrors the question of the identity of Nympha and Junia. Some have argued that the Elect Lady is a church. However, "Clement of Alexandria (ca. 200) wrote that the second letter of John was addressed 'to a certain Babylonian woman named Electa,' which signifies the election of the holy church."[17] The second letter of John is dated between 90 and 120 C.E. Thus, a century later, church Father Clement of Alexandria believed the letter was written to a woman.

And there are more women. Claudia sends greetings to Timothy in Second Timothy 4:21. Although unnamed, Paul's sister is found in Acts 23:16. There are the great numbers of women who are added to the Lord in Acts 5:14, are baptized in Acts 8:12, dragged off to prison in Acts 8:3 and 8:22, and are under threat of being arrested in Acts 9:2. There are the leading women and women of high standing who became believers in Acts 17:4 and 17:12. And there are the widows

---

17 Winter, *Woman Word*, 287.

Tabatha the disciple cares for in Joppa, as do the seven leading men in Jerusalem.

Those who want to argue that women did not prophesy in the early church will find a way to deny Phillip's prophetic daughters and the other women who are called prophets in the Bible. Those who want to argue that Phoebe was not a deacon or that Junia was a man will find a way to do so. Those who want to argue that women were not leaders in the churches which met in their homes, like Mary in Jerusalem or Lydia in Philippi and Nympha in Colossae, will develop an argument. Those who want to dispute the evidence that communities of women gathered for worship without the presence of men, like the community of women where Paul met Lydia, will find a way. Those who want to believe that when God is quoted as saying, "In the last days I will pour out my spirit on all flesh and your sons and your daughters will prophesy" (NRSV) means something different for men than for women, will continue to believe and try to convince others.

I believe in a God who pours out God's spirit equally on women and men. Those who want to argue that the teaching of Priscilla in Acts 18:24–28 is less significant than that of Paul's in Acts 28:23 will develop their argument. Paul was under house arrest. He was not teaching in public. Churches were in homes, not in the public sphere. Priscilla, like Paul, was teaching in the only forum open to them at the time.

There are more women's biblical stories to tell. However, I have limited my scope to the women with some direct connection to Jesus. As is evident from the above discussion, there were women active in the missionary work of the early church. Unfortunately, most of the stories about the individual women in the formative years of the church have been lost to us.

Even the stories of women in our own short American history are not generally remembered. Who remembers the first European women to settle in the colonies (Anne Forrest and Anne Buras), or the first American woman ordained a minister (Antoinette Blackwell in

1835), or the names of the women responsible for securing the right to vote for American women (Susan B. Anthony and Elizabeth Cady Stanton among many others)? Mary Baker Eddy was the founder of Christian Science, and Clara Barton founded the American Red Cross. Generally, these women's names and stories are not taught in our American history classes, just as the names and stories of biblical women have not been recorded in the Bible or taught in our pulpits and Sunday Schools. We know women were there, whether or not their names and contributions are recorded and recognized. Thankfully, in these writings of Paul, we get a glimpse into their importance and their work.

The erasure of women continues today. In May of 2011, the White House released a picture taken in the Situation Room. Two women, Secretary of State Hillary Clinton and National Director of Counterterrorism, Audrey Tomason, were in the picture. When the ultra-orthodox Jewish newspaper *Der Tzitung* published the picture, Secretary Clinton and Director Tomason had been photoshopped out. Their historic presence and importance had been erased. If the only bit of information to survive for two thousand years depicting American history in 2011 was that paper, one might assume that the American government excluded women.

This illustrates what has happened to biblical women. They have been erased. The Rabbi Jason Miller, writing for *The Jewish Week*, explained, "The Hasidic newspaper will not intentionally include any image of women in the paper because it could be considered sexually suggestive."[18] Credulity is stretched to find anything sexually suggestive about this picture. Secretary Clinton is dressed in a suit with long sleeves, a high neck and her hand over her mouth, a look of horror on her face. Director Tomason's face is all that is seen in the back of the photo. As this example demonstrates, even though we do

[18] Jason Miller, "Hasidic Newspaper Photoshops Hillary Clinton from Iconic Photo," *The Jewish Week,* May 8, 2011. http://www.thejewishweek.com/blogs/jewish_techs/hasidic_newspsper_photoshop_hillary_clinton_iconic_photo.

not want to believe it, women are actually erased. There are those in every faith tradition who would seek to limit and erase women, but we know women were there.

In the letter to the Galatians, written in the middle of the first century, Paul challenges the prayer Jewish men recited in which they thanked God that they were not born slaves, Gentiles or women. Galatians 3:26–29 states that we are all children of God through faith in Jesus. We are neither Jew nor Greek, slave nor free, male nor female but all one, all heirs by virtue of our baptism.

Gentiles, slaves and women were seen as inferior or polluted and not able to come before God. "As F. F. Bruce notes, the pious expressed such gratitude because these other persons 'were disqualified from several religious privileges which were open to free Jewish males.'"[19]

Paul is declaring that the social and economic distinctions between slave and master, Gentile and Jew, woman and man have no place in the new Christian movement and no place in the church. Women, by virtue of their baptism, have direct access to God and equal partnership and responsibilities in the church.

Other writings attributed to Paul are used to limit the full inclusion and participation of women in the church. Most notably, First Corinthians 11:3–16; 14:33–36; Colossians 3:18–19; Ephesians 5:21–33; First Timothy 2:9–14; and First Peter 3:1–7. The gospel of Jesus means good news, not good news for men and status quo for women. These verses and the resulting attitudes they engender are insulting! Men as the image and reflection of God? What a powerful position to claim for one's self and one's gender. Are all men the image and reflection of God, and if not, who gets to decide who is and who isn't? Women are not the image and reflection of men. How comforting for men to claim that woman was made for the sake of

---

[19] F. F. Bruce, *Commentary on Galatians,* New International Greek Testament Commentary (Grand Rapids: Eerdmans, 1982), p. 187; quoted in Stanley Grenz with Denise Muir Khesbo, *Women in the Church: A Biblical Theology of Women in Ministry* (Downers Grove: InterVarsity Press, 1995), 100.

man. What happened to the woman created simultaneously with the man in Genesis 1:27? Women have much to say in church for the edification of the church. It is not good news to be told that women must be subject to their husbands. That is simply archaic! These were the beliefs about women in the Greco-Roman world of the first and second centuries. Even with all the insistence in many churches that First Corinthians 11:3–16 dictates a submissive role for women, the instructions for veiling is virtually ignored.

There is no evidence that these were the beliefs of Jesus. On the contrary, Jesus advocated a radical new social order in which women and men participated equally. The 2006 and the 2008 first-place winners of the Baptist History and Heritage Society preaching contest were Courtney Kreuger and Martha Kearse. It does not make sense that God would bestow the gift of teaching or preaching on a woman and not want her to use it for the edification of the church. Women have different experiences of the world by virtue of being women. If women's voices and experiences are silenced, half of God's self-revelation, half of the human experience of God, is lost to the church. Men have much they can learn about women's experiences of the world and women's relationship with our Creator.

Paul's first letter to the Corinthians is a situational letter. "Chloe's people" reported to Paul that members of the assembly were quarreling, apparently about several issues, because the assembly also sent a letter to Paul asking him to address their questions. In First Corinthians 11:3–16, Paul writes to address *their* issues.

There are numerous ways to interpret this chapter which do not require the subordination of women in the home, in society, or in the church. The commentary for this section in *The New Oxford Annotated Bible* is titled "Arguments concerning hair style." (NRSV) Paul talks both about hair styles and veils. Most North American Christian women no longer adhere to the instruction to veil their heads or conform to first-century hair styles and do not shave their heads in lieu of a veil. Paul was addressing a style of the time, not dictating the way women should wear their hair or veil their heads for all time. Yet these verses are used to defend the subordination of women in the church and the home.

Verse three says that God is the head of Christ, Christ is the head of the man, and the husband, not any man but the husband, is the head of the wife. In the Greco-Roman culture of Corinth, women had little to no authority. It is quite likely that the male members of the Corinthian church were also powerless members of the larger society. First Corinthians 1:27–29 says, "But God chose what is foolish in the world to shame the wise; God chose what is weak in the world to shame the strong; God chose what is low and despised in the world, things that are not, to reduce to nothing things that are, so that no one might boast in the presence of God." (NRSV) Paul describes the Corinthians as foolish, weak, lowly nothings.

Although they appear to have no authority in society, they do have authority in the church. If Christ derives authority from God, God placed no restrictions on the authority of Christ. The members of the community derive their authority in the community from Christ. The female members of the community have authority, and the male members must allow the women in the community the authority they have been given. There is no subordination in the God/Christ relationship. Neither should there be subordination in the male/female relationship. Women are praying and prophesying in the church as are men. Paul does not require that they stop their prophetic activity.

Another interpretation of First Corinthians 1:27–29 could be that because the women are viewed as foolish, weak, low and despised by men, they put to shame the men who think of themselves as wise, strong, elevated and respected, so that the men cannot boast.

But what if the word translated as "head" did not mean "authority"? "It is likely, as many argue, that 'head here means source' and not rank or authority."[20] If a more accurate translation of head is source,

---

[20] Newsom and Ringe, 326.

perhaps Paul is referring to his argument in verse eight that woman was taken from man. He argues from Genesis 2:22, the second creation story in Genesis. In that story, woman is made by God from the rib of the first human. In the first story of creation, found in Genesis 1:17, male and female humans are created simultaneously in the image and likeness of God. This story is repeated in Genesis 5:1–2. They are both the reflection of God. One was not made for the other. They are both blessed, both commissioned to procreate and care for creation, and both are part of the creation which God proclaims as "very good." God, not man, is the source of the woman. The man is simply a vessel God uses to create the woman. In either case, woman is the reflection of God's action in creation and not the reflection of man. She is the final and ultimate act of creation, needed to complete the incomplete first human. Woman is the only creature created from a living being and not created from the dust of the earth.

In chapter six, Paul addresses the issue of fornication and relationships with prostitutes in the Corinthian church. I am persuaded that Paul is addressing the male members of the church. Historically, men, not women, are the most frequent customers of prostitutes.

In chapter seven, Paul goes to great length to answer questions the Corinthians raised in their letter to him. We do not know the questions, but the answer concerned sexual relationships between members of the Corinthian church. Corinth was known for prostitution and sexual corruption. "Corinth offered another attractive feature for Paul: its long-standing reputation for immorality and licentiousness."[21] Is this the problem Paul was addressing?

Veils were an article of clothing for women in the public sphere. Men were accustomed to seeing veiled women. Is Paul's constraint on women to veil themselves because the men in the church are unable

---

[21] Dan Cole, "Into the Heart of Paganism: Why did Paul, the traveling missionary, set down roots in Corinth and Ephesus?" *Christian History*, XIV, no. 47 (1995), 22.

to control their passions around the unveiled women? They seem to need correction in regard to fornication and prostitutes.

In some Muslim traditions, women are required to veil themselves to hide their features from men who are not family members. If a woman is covered, her physical beauty is less obvious. The assumption is that men will not be attracted to a woman whose beauty they cannot see. Their passions toward the woman will not be inflamed.

The women have taken seriously the assurance of their baptism. There is no longer slave nor free, Gentile nor Jew, male nor female. The racial, social and economic barriers have been removed, for all are one in Christ. It appears Paul is trying to control a problem that has surfaced in the church in Corinth by asking women to return to the cultural status quo. If this is the case, the women are being blamed for the improprieties of the men. We see a parallel of this in our own culture, when rape victims are blamed for the rape.

Corinthians worshiped Greek, Roman and Egyptian gods and goddesses: Poseidon, Aphrodite, Athena, Hera and Hermes, among others. It could have been that the women were practicing their new faith as they would have as members of one of these cults. "Flowing and unbound hair was also found in the Isis cult, which had a major center in Corinth."[22] Perhaps Paul's call for tied-up hair and/or veils was something he was teaching the Corinthians about worship that was in contrast to what they had experienced in the past. Jewish women who had become Christians would have had no experience with that kind of ecstatic worship and thus not need the correction the Corinthians did.

In verse ten Paul seems to reverse his previous argument. He says that a woman should have authority on her head because of the angels. He also says that men and women are interdependent on each other

[22] Elizabeth Schussler-Fiorenza, *In Memory of Her: A Feminist Theological Reconstruction of Christian Origins* (New York: Crossroad, 1990), 227.

in the Lord, the reason being that man now comes through woman. He asks his readers to judge for themselves. Is it right for women to pray without a veil? He then appeals to nature, but it is not really an appeal to nature. Hair grows unless, of course, you go bald! It is really an appeal to the styles of the Greco-Roman world. It is fashion, personal preference and cultural custom which dictate the length of hair on men or women, not nature.

Finally, Paul abandons his argument and confesses in verse sixteen that, "We have no such customs, nor do the churches of God." (NRSV) We do not know what the problems were in the Corinthian church. However, there are possibilities for interpreting *The Bible* to answer questions about the first century which do not demand the subjugation of women in the twenty-first century.

I will not go to such length in my observations of the other distressing verses and inconsistencies in the Epistles. There is much debate about whether these verses are authentically Paul or whether they were added by later generations who were actively attempting to limit the participation of women in the church. *The New Oxford Annotated Bible* says this about the verses examined above: "Because 11:3–16 interrupts an otherwise easy movement from 11:2 to 11:17–18:17, and because the vocabulary and content of the passage are strange for Paul, but resemble those of deutero-Pauline letters such as Colossians, Ephesians, and First and Second Timothy, it may be a later interpolation." (NRSV)

Briefly, in First Corinthians 14:34–36, women are commanded to be silent in church and subordinate, as the law says. Are these really the words of Paul? Why would Paul appeal to the law? Is it the law of the Greco-Roman culture or Jewish law? As Christians, we are not under Jewish law, as Paul has argued vehemently. In Romans 3:21–22 Paul says, "But now, apart from law, the righteousness of God has been disclosed, and is attested by the law and the prophets the righteousness of God through faith in Jesus Christ." (NRSV)

In verses 23–24 Paul speaks of the whole church coming together and all speaking and all prophesying. In verse 26 Paul says each one has a hymn, a lesson, a revelation for building up the assembly. This does not imply a hierarchy but a community of equals. We have already seen that women were praying and prophesying in the Corinthian Church. If Paul were trying to silence women, why did he not do so in chapter eleven, instead of discussing their attire and hair style? "These statements silencing women in the assembly are found in two different places in the ancient manuscripts, between 14:33 and 14:36, and after 14:40 they may be a marginal gloss later interpolated into the text; similar wording occurs in First Timothy 2:11–12." (NRSV) It is possible that these are not the words of Paul, but of a later interpreter of Paul's letters, who had an agenda to silence women. No matter who actually wrote those words of silence, they have been used to limit women's participation in the church.

First Timothy, Second Timothy, Titus, Colossians, and Ephesians are writings which modern scholars suspect were not written by Paul but by a disciple of Paul at a later date. The Roman Catholic and Southern Baptist churches do not allow women to be priests or pastors. The reason given on the *Baptist Faith and Message* website is "The office of pastor is limited to men as qualified by scripture."[23] The site contains a specific reference to First Timothy 2:11–12. "From the late second century to the nineteenth, Pauline authorship of the three Pastoral Epistles went unchallenged. Since then, the attribution of these letters to Paul has been questioned. Most scholars are convinced that Paul could not have been responsible for the vocabulary and style, the concept of church organization or the theological expressions found in these letters." (NAB) It is from these letters that we find most of the verses restricting women to subordinate roles. Regardless

---

[23] Staff of the Executive Committee of the SBC, "Southern Baptist and Women Pastors," *Baptist2Baptist*. April 10, 2011. http://www.baptist2baptist.net.

of authorship, these letters are in the Bible and have influenced the formation of Christianity.

Colossians 3:18 commands wives to be subject to their husbands and children to obey their parents. In verse 22, slaves are told to obey their earthly masters and in verse 4:1, masters are told to treat their slaves justly and fairly. The wisdom of children's obedience to their parents is unquestioned. It is the responsibility of parents to patiently, lovingly and kindly correct their children. However, subjugation and slavery do not distinguish the community of believers from the Greco-Roman household. Households based on patriarchal rule considered women as property.

In Ephesians 5:21, all the members of the community are encouraged to be subject to one another. Following these edifying words, wives are asked to subjugate themselves to their husbands using the argument of headship. This is softened with a very extended call to husbands to love their wives as they love themselves and wives are now asked to respect instead of be subject to their husbands. And as in Colossians, children and slaves are exhorted to be obedient. Admonitions for master and slave are generally not used to develop church doctrine and practice. It is anachronistic to continue to use verses that command the subjugation of women in the church, home or larger society.

First Timothy does not appear to be good news for women. In 2:9 women are told how to dress, how to wear their hair, and not to wear jewelry. In general, these restrictions are not employed to limit women in the church today. What is used is 2:11–15. These verses instruct women to be submissive and silent, with no authority over men. An interpretation of the second creation story in Genesis is used to qualify this silent submission. Then the author says something very strange. Women will be saved through bearing children. If women are saved by bearing children, why do mothers need Jesus? If the author is Paul, he has completely reversed the doctrine of salvation found in

Romans 1:19. "For I am not ashamed of the gospel; it is the power of God for salvation to everyone who has faith, to the Jew first and also to the Greek." (NRSV)

In First Timothy 5:13–14, women are stereotypically depicted as idle gossips and busybodies. Young widows are instructed to marry, have children and keep house. "Daily life centered on what can be called the 'family household,' which was the basic unit of society."[24] In First Corinthians 7:8, Paul encourages the unmarried and widows to stay unmarried as he is. If these are the words of Paul, he has reversed himself again.

Finally, the question of authority. From the beginning of the church, the Spirit was poured out on men and women equally. Acts 2:4, "All of them were filled with the Holy Spirit and began to speak in other languages, as the Spirit gave them ability." (NRSV) Is the Spirit of God limited by the gender of the body it fills? With the exception of the pastoral letters, Paul writes to churches, not to the leaders of the churches, although he greets some of those who have been active in the work of the communities.

According to the website *Early Christian Writings,* the first letter to Timothy was written between 100 and 150 C.E. That is seventy or more years after the life of Jesus and thirty some years after the death of Paul. It appears that the model of inclusivity which Jesus practiced had begun to give way to the larger cultural ideas of women: cultural ideas that were heavily influenced by the philosophies of Plato and Aristotle. Plato did not believe that women had souls, and Aristotle believed that women were defective by nature. Jesus talked to women in public and in private; he taught women and traveled with women. The call for women's silence and submission mirrors more closely the culture Jesus defied rather than the community Jesus modeled.

First Peter, like First Timothy, instructs slaves to accept the authority of their masters and wives to accept the authority their

---

24 Newsom and Ringe, 246.

husbands. This letter also tells women how to wear their hair and how to dress. Biblical writers interpret earlier biblical writings, and we are often deeply affected by these interpretations. For example, First Peter 3 says that holy women of old accepted the authority of their husbands and that Sarah obeyed Abraham. If we are not thinking for ourselves we might take that at face value. But Sarah did not obey Abraham. Sarah made the choice to give Hagar to Abraham. Sarah sent Hagar away when Hagar was pregnant, telling Abraham, basically, "this is all your fault." When Sarah was angry and wanted Hagar and Ishmael sent away, Abraham did not want them to go. God instructed Abraham to listen to the voice of Sarah so Hagar and Ishmael were sent away. The writer of First Peter has interpreted the actions of Sarah as obedience, but this does not sound like submissive obedience. Rebekah tricked Isaac into giving Jacob the blessing of the first born. This does not sound like accepting her husband's authority. Leah and Rachel were consulted by Jacob when he wanted to leave their father and return to his homeland. They decided, on at least one occasion, who Jacob was going to sleep with. Again, this does not sound like submissively accepting their husband's authority. The writer of First Peter put forward his interpretation of Sarah and other biblical women, as instruction for the audience to whom he was writing. We do not have to accept his interpretation but can engage the stories of biblical women and develop our own interpretations.

Conclusion

The Bible's words and interpretations have been used throughout history to justify a group or an individual's point of view. It has been used to justify wars, slavery, polygamist marriage and the subjugation of women, to name a few. King James 1 of England, the same king who gave us *The King James Bible,* used 2 Samuel 8:10–20 to justify his claim to the divine right of the monarchy. In the document *The Trew Law of Free Monarchies,* he states, "I will set downe the trew grounds, whereupon I am to build, out of the Scriptures, since Monarchie is the trew paterne of Divinity, as I have already said: next, from the fundamental Lawes of our own Kingdome, which nearest must concerne us: thirdly, from the law of Nature, by divers similitudes drawne out of the same."[25]

Who can argue with a government and a head of state which derives authority from God and the laws of nature? But the Puritans did argue, and they left England. It served slave holders and racists well to quote the Bible and nature to defend slavery and segregation. But many did argue, and institutional slavery and segregation have been abolished in the United States. It serves men and some women well to quote the Bible and nature to argue for the subordination of women. But, many do argue that it is not divinely ordained or the law of nature for women to be subordinated to men.

I have always found it remarkable that the church is not credited with having church mothers in the same way it is credited with having church fathers. But the book of Acts and the Epistles reveal that there were church mothers who established churches in their cities and who nourished the churches in their homes. Women like Mary the mother of John Mark were instrumental in founding and developing the early church. Women were disciples, as the example of Tabatha demonstrates. Women were teachers and ministers, as the example of Priscilla validates. Women were praying and prophesying in the church, as First Corinthians and the prophetic daughters of Philip establish.

Adding the suffix "ess" or "ette" to a word as in waitress, hostess, deaconess, or suffragette, diminishes the importance of the person or the task. The suffix "ess" denotes the actions of women, and "ette" describes something small. At the church in which I grew up, the deacons stood up front on Sunday mornings, said the prayers and served the communion. The deaconesses prepared the communion and then cleaned up the communion after church. Except, of course,

[25] Mark Kishlansky, Patrick Geary and Patricia O'Brien, *Civilization in the West,* 6th ed., vol. I (New York: Pearson Education, Inc., 2007), D-43.

on Women's Sunday, when women prepared the communion, served the communion and cleaned up the communion after church.

There is no pejorative suffix added to the Greek word *diakonos.* It is the English translators who have diminished the ministry of Lydia by translating her *diakonos* as "deaconess" or "servant." We know women were there praying, prophesying, establishing and supporting churches, and so much more.

Chapter Eight

More than Bible Study

Where to Find the Story of Our Biblical Mother Eve

I struggled with including Eve and her story and considered not including her at all. However, as a consequence of the centuries of wounds inflicted on women as a result of the interpretations of Eve's story, she deserves attention. Beginning with First Corinthians 11:8, in which the writer uses his interpretation of Genesis 11:21–23 to state that woman was made from and for the sake of man, the story of Eve has been used to limit, insult or subordinate women. Bathsheba is often remembered as the woman who seduced King David. She is not usually remembered as the woman wronged by King David. Similarly Eve is remembered as the first woman, the first sinner and the first to lead a man astray. She is not remembered as a curious, intelligent, naive but decisive woman. As a child growing up in church, I was encouraged to be more like Jesus, which I equated with being more like God. I often questioned why Eve's decision to eat a fruit, which would make her more like God, was a terrible thing. The story Eve tells below is reconstructed from the second story of Creation found in Genesis 2:4–3:24.

Eve Tells Her Story

> "When I saw that the fruit was beautiful and that it would make me wise, I ate some and gave some to my partner who ate it also." (Eve in Genesis 3:6)

It was another day in paradise. My partner was with me while I talked with the serpent. The creature asked what limits God had put on what we could eat and what we could not. I said we could not eat of the Tree of Life or the Tree of the Knowledge of Good and Evil, because if we did we would die. Well, the serpent told me I would not die but become like God, knowing good and evil. I longed to be more like God! I longed for wisdom! I could see that the fruit of the tree was beautiful and I thought eating it would make me wise. So I tried it. I gave some to my partner also. He accepted it without question.

The instant we ate the fruit, our eyes were opened. There is so much about being human that we had not understood. The serpent was right; we did not die, but God was saddened that we now had knowledge of good and evil. We were no longer like children. God questioned our actions. I admitted I had been tricked by the serpent and had eaten the fruit. My partner blamed God for my very presence. He took no responsibility for his own actions.

Our sexual knowledge had changed. Before we ate the fruit, we were not ashamed of our naked bodies. Now we were ashamed and wanted to cover ourselves. As long as we were like children, we would never have children. With our new knowledge, we would have children of our own. I was told what it would be like to have children, that even with that pain I would continue to love my partner, but he would attempt to rule over me. I did not know what "rule over" could mean. God was the only one to whom we were accountable. Was rule of one over another a consequence of our new knowledge?

We were partners. We were the same flesh and bone. What could "rule over" possibly mean?

God made clothes for us and sent us from the garden. The lives we had created for ourselves, full of children and work, could never happen in the confines of the garden.

Observations on Eve's Story

What do we believe about the creation stories? Was all of creation accomplished by the voice of God, as described in the first creation story found in Genesis 1:1–2:3? Or, does the second story of creation, found in Genesis 2:4–25, in which God uses dirt to form a human, the plants and the animals, describe the method of creation?

Megan McKenna, an author, theologian and storyteller, says, "All stories are true. Some of them actually happened."[1] My understanding of this statement is that there is truth in every story, whether or not the story being told was an historical event. Is Eve an historical figure? Are the two different stories of creation actual, historical, literal events, or are they stories told by an ancient people to explain the world they experienced around them?

In the first story of creation, humans are created male and female at the same moment, in the image and likeness of God. Their creation is the climax of God's creative activity. They are given every plant and every tree for food, with no restrictions. In this story, neither the man nor the woman has a voice. The creation is completed in six days and God is said to rest on the seventh day. Why does God need rest? Most likely, this is an explanation of the Jewish religious practice of Sabbath rest. There is no mention of a garden in the first story of creation.

In the second story, creation is not completed in six days; in fact, no time line is given. Eve is not called Eve until she leaves the garden

---

1 Megan McKenna, lecture, Religious Education Congress of the Archdiocese of Los Angeles.

at the end of the second story. She is named Eve because now she will be a mother, the mother of all humanity. The Hebrew word for Eve, *hawwah,* means life or living. In the second story of creation, the first human is formed from dust before any other living creature. God appears to struggle to create a companion appropriate for the first human. Out of the ground, God creates every animal of the field and every bird of the air, but a companion appropriate for the first earth creature is not found. Finally, God creates the woman. She is the climax of God's creative activity, created from living flesh, not from the dust. In this story, God does not rest, but walks around in the garden with the first couple. The first human is given all the trees in the garden for food except the Tree of the Knowledge of Good and Evil and the Tree of Life. If we interpret this story literally and chronologically, the woman was not yet formed when the instruction not to eat the fruit of those trees is given. How did she know God's instructions about the forbidden fruit? Was it the responsibility of the first human to tell her, or was she cognizant in the first human, something more than a rib? If we believe this is an historical, factual account of creation, perhaps the first human was an androgynous creature, having both male and female anatomy. Perhaps the separating that happens in Genesis 2:22 is not a rib but female aspects of the first human, separated from the male aspects of the first human.

Some would like to combine these two stories into one creation story, as the two nativity stories are combined in Christmas celebrations. But they are separate stories from different sources. The first story is from the priestly (P) source. "The P source employs the divine epithet El Shaddai (often translated 'God Almighty') in Genesis; God emerges in this source as an even more transcendent being."[2] The second story is from the Yahwist (J) source. "J is characterized by the use of the name Yahweh for God, by a down-to-earth style, and

[2] Newsom and Ringe, 11.

by a theology that allows God certain closeness to the human realm; for example, God walks in the garden (Gen.3:8)."[3]

Genesis 3:1–7 is often employed to justify the subjugation of women. The author of First Timothy interprets this chapter to restrict women's teaching and authority. Yet the woman is the active agent in the story found in the third chapter of Genesis. She is the leader, not the follower. She is the one having a conversation with the clever, talking serpent. When the woman reaches out for wisdom and knowledge, she offers some to the man. He accepts her gift passively. He offers no resistance. She wanted to be wise; she wanted to be like God. Most interpreters focus on the disobedience of Eve, ignoring the culpability of the man with her. She is not being ruled over by the man but is taking the initiative. She is human, not divine. She had not yet eaten the fruit of the knowledge of good and evil. She did not know the difference between right and wrong.

Eve is not cursed as a result of her actions. The serpent and the ground are cursed in Genesis 3:14 and 3:17b. Eve is told she will have pain in childbirth and her husband will rule over her in Genesis 3:16. If a child is told not to touch something hot, and the child touches the object, reasonable, loving people check to see how bad the burn is, comfort the child and medicate the burn. We do not punish the child, as God is reported doing in chapter three. The ancient people saw that women had pain in childbirth; the ancient people worked hard to produce food, and men were in control of women and their reproductive abilities. These stories explain why life was the way it was for an ancient people. It is not a prescription for the way it must be forever.

Many women receive medication to make childbirth less painful. There are, however, some men who do not want their wives to receive pain medication based on Genesis 3:16. In a newspaper column I

---

3 *Ibid.*, 11.

read years ago, the husband of a young woman told her she could not have an epidural or pain medication "because childbirth is supposed to be painful. It is a judgment on women because Eve ate the apple." Further, the young woman "is terrified of going through the birth without medication, but does not want to upset her husband because of his temper." This is spousal abuse and negates the sacrifice of Jesus. Galatians 5:1 says, "For freedom Christ has set us free." (NRSV) It is difficult to understand how a man who calls himself a Christian would want to see his wife suffer needlessly. Ephesians 5:33 says "Each of you, however, should love his wife as himself, and a wife should respect her husband." (NRSV) How does a woman respect a man who would require her to suffer needlessly?

We do not take literally the requirement that all men should work in the field producing food, as stated in Genesis 3:17–19. There are certainly many men and women who do not work as farmers, toiling in the field to feed themselves and their families. Farming is an honorable profession, but men and women work at any number of jobs aside from "tilling the ground." Many systems of oppression have changed. Women are routinely given medication to alleviate the pain of childbirth and institutionalized slavery and segregation have been eliminated from American culture. Unfortunately, slavery continues to persist in the United States and globally. If we believe that the life and example of Jesus was to redeem humanity, then it is our responsibility to change systems of oppression. Instead of being blamed as the architect of original sin, Eve should be praised for her willingness to take a risk and bring wisdom and knowledge to humanity. Civilization as we know it could not have existed or developed in "the garden."

One anthropological theory for the story of the first couple leaving the garden is a description of civilization evolving from hunter/gatherer to an agricultural society. It reflects nostalgia for an easier way of life. "Is it a coincidence? The opening chapters of Genesis depict situations that parallel modern anthropological theories about the transition from a gathering/hunting society to an agricultural/ herding society."[4]

What do we believe about the fruit Eve ate? The husband, in the example above, seems to believe that Eve ate an apple. She ate the fruit of the Tree of the Knowledge of Good and Evil. The text says nothing about an apple. She was encouraged to eat the fruit by a clever, talking serpent. A talking serpent makes a literal interpretation of Genesis 3:1–5 very difficult to digest. Some have interpreted the serpent as the devil, but the Bible says that it was a wild animal or a beast of the field. In the ancient Near East and elsewhere, snakes represented not only female wisdom but the goddess. "Snakes were a symbol in the ancient world of wisdom, fertility, and immortality." (NRSV) The writers of Genesis are challenging the religions of the people around them. Genesis describes the creation of the heavens, specifically to emphasize that the sun, moon and stars are part of creation and not to be worshipped. "The principal divinity of the people of Canaan was the Goddess, and associated with the Goddess is the serpent. This is the symbol of the mystery of life which the male-god-oriented group rejected. In other words, there is a historical rejection of the Mother Goddess implied in the story of the Garden of Eden."[5]

Adam is created male and female, by the word of God in Genesis 1:27. In this case Adam is not the proper name of a male human being. Rather, it is humankind who are created in the image of God, male and female. "The Hebrew word for man (Adam) is collective, referring not to an individual but to humanity as a whole."[6] (RSV)

In Genesis 2:7 a human is again created. This time it is a singular human created from the dust of the earth. The designation male or female is not stated. There are those who would argue that because

---

4 Eleanor Ferris Beach and Frederic L. Pryor, "How Did Adam and Eve Make a Living?" *Bible Review* XI, no.2 (April 1995): 38–42.

5 Joseph Campbell and Bill Moyers, *The Power of Myth* (New York: Doubleday, 1988), 48.

6 "Humanity" replaces "men" in the quote above.

the verse says God breathed into *his* nostrils, the gender of this single human is male. "Neutral pronouns did not exist in Hebrew. But, as observed in Genesis 1:27, where man is created both male and female, male pronouns are used to identify and erase women. We have the same situation in the English language. Often, the human race is identified as *man* or *mankind.* On July 20, 1969, astronaut Neil Armstrong stepped onto the moon. His now-famous quote is, "That's one small step for man, one giant leap for mankind." Womankind was invisible from this historic moment. It would be another fourteen years before Sally Ride would be the first woman in space.

Women and girls are called guys and dudes. On a recent trip to Victoria's Secret, I heard a young woman's voice say, "Dude, look at this bra." I turned, expecting to see a young woman and a young man. Instead, I saw two young women. Our culture has taught them that it is acceptable to think and speak of themselves in male generic language.

Information gets lost in translation. "The word play on Heb 'adam' (human being; here translated 'man' [cf. 1:26]) and 'adaman' arable land; here *ground*) introduces a motif characteristic of this tradition: the relation of human kind to the soil from which it was formed." (NRSV) So why is this important? Because a theology of women's subordination has been developed from the interpretation of Adam as a male human being, a man who needed a helper. But Jesus is not credited with developing a theology of women's subordination. Jesus is quoted in Matthew 19:4–6 as saying, "Have you not read that the one who made them at the beginning 'made them male and female,' and said, 'For this reason a man shall leave his father and mother and be joined to his wife, and the two shall become one flesh'?" (NRSV) Mark 10:6–9 says, "But from the beginning of creation, 'God made them male and female.' 'For this reason a man shall leave his father and mother and be joined to his wife, and the two shall become one flesh.' So they are no longer two, but one flesh." (NRSV) Jesus does not insist on the submission or subjugation of women. Rather, Jesus calls for equality of the man and the woman created male and female in the image of God from the beginning.

Church Fathers

What the "Church Fathers" had to say about women is shocking! Based on the words of these men, the church is a very abusive family, indeed. Just as the first man is said to blame both the woman and God for his action of eating the fruit of the Tree of the Knowledge of Good and Evil, church fathers have blamed women for sin in the world. They have used their words and positions of power to scapegoat women for their own sexual aggression and shortcomings.

Tertullian, a second-century church father, told women, "And do you not know that you are (each) an Eve? The sentence of God on this sex of yours lives in this age: the guilt must of necessity live too. You are the Devil's gateway: you are the unsealer of that (forbidden) tree: you are the first deserter of the divine law: you are she who persuaded him whom the devil was not valiant enough to attack. You destroyed so easily God's image, man. On account of your desert—that is, death—even the Son of God had to die. And do you think about adorning yourself over and above your tunics of skin?"[7]

Reading this attack on women, I am reminded of the mob that brought a woman accused of adultery to Jesus in John's gospel. Let the one among you who is sinless cast the first stone. Tertullian seems to believe that Eve was conversing with the devil instead of a crafty serpent. Tertullian seems to ignore the fact that woman was created in the image of God, and he disregards the fact that the man, whom he is defending, did not argue with the woman about eating the fruit, but passively took and ate. He also seems not to notice that the man blames both God and the woman for his actions. Like the mob that brings the woman to Jesus, the man caught with the woman in

---

7 Marg Mowczko, "Misogynist Quotes from Church Fathers and Theologians," *Newlife*, October 2, 2013. http://www.newlife.id.au/misogynist-quotes-from-church-fathers/.

the act of adultery is let off the hook; only the woman is blamed. In Tertullian's argument, only the woman is guilty of sin; the man is blameless. Tertullian forgets that woman is not cursed by God. Does Tertullian think he has lived a blameless life, or is that the fault of women also? If sin is blamed on the act of one woman, then men can successfully scapegoat their shortfalls on women. I choose not to be the reason for the sins of any man. They can take responsibility for themselves!

St. Clement of Alexandria, a second-century Greek Church father, believed, "Every woman should be filled with shame by the thought that she is a woman . . . the consciousness of their own nature must evoke feelings of shame."[8] St. Jerome wrote, "Woman is the root of all evil."[9] Clement and Jerome seem not to have read the first chapter of Genesis in which the creation of woman is declared very good. What nonsense!

St. John Chrysostom, the Bishop of Constantinople, the same John who wrote so glowingly of Junia the apostle, wrote, "God maintained the order of each sex by dividing the business of life into two parts, and assigned the more necessary and beneficial aspect to the man and the less important, inferior matter to the woman."[10]

St. Augustine, a doctor of the church and the bishop of Hippo, wrote, "I don't see what sort of help woman was created to provide man with, if one excluded procreation. If woman is not given to man for help in bearing children, for what help could she be? To till the earth together? If help were needed for that, man would have been a better help for man. The same goes for comfort in solitude. How much more pleasure is it for life and conversation when two friends live together than when a man and a woman cohabitate?"[11]

---

8 *Ibid.*

9 *Ibid.*

10 *Ibid.*

11 *Ibid.*

St. Augustine is considered by many to be a great father of the church, yet he had deplorable attitudes toward women. Further, he seems to have developed a theology which questions the goodness and perfection of God in God's act of creation.

Origen believed, "Men should not sit and listen to a woman . . . even if she says admirable things, or even saintly things, that is of little consequence, since it came from the mouth of a woman."[12]

St. Thomas Aquinas from the thirteenth century believed, "Good order would have been wanting in the human family if some were not governed by others wiser than themselves. So by such a kind of subjection woman is naturally subject to man, because in men the discretion of reason predominates."[13]

In the Bible, the Wisdom of God is personified as a woman. Proverbs 4:6 says, "Get wisdom; get insight: do not forget, nor turn away firm the words of my mouth. Do not forsake her, and she will keep you; love her, and she will guard you." (NRSV) Yet St. Thomas Aquinas believed that a woman is deficient. In this example of male "reason," the wisdom of women, which women know women possess, is ignored for an argument from nature. There are many men and women who appear to possess neither reason nor common sense. Shall wise women govern and subjugate those we believe less wise than ourselves? Women are not deficient! We were created in the image and likeness of God! Woman, the climax of God's creative action in both stories of creation, was created for full human dignity, not subjugation.

The German inquisitors Heinrich Kraemer and Jacob Sprenger of the fifteenth century wrote in the *Malleus Maleficarum (The Witch Hammer),* that women are only imperfect animals and crooked but men belong to a privileged sex from whose midst Christ emerged. This is actually one of the nicer statements made about women in the

---

12 *Ibid.*

13 Melly, "Misogyny in the Church-EXPOSED." *Geo Cities.* October 16, 2009 http://www.oocities.org/melly4JC/misogyny.html.

Malleus Maleficarum. This document was used as a tool to prosecute, condemn and murder more than 48,000 women. The entire *Malleus Maleficarum* is a ferocious assault on women. The authors state that Christ emerged from the "privileged sex." With this statement I would have to agree. Jesus, whom we call The Christ, emerged from a woman. If we believe in the "virgin birth," man had nothing to do with it.

Martin Luther preached, "Remember that you are a woman, and that this work of God in you is pleasing to him. Trust joyfully in his will, and let him have his way with you. Work with all your might to bring forth the child. Should it mean your death, then depart happily, for you will die in a noble deed and in subservience to God."[14] The life of women giving birth was apparently of no importance to the father of Protestantism. I do not believe, however, that he can claim to know that a woman's death in childbirth is a "noble deed" and "pleasing" to God.

This section was heart wrenching to research and write, yet the quotes listed above barely scratch the surface. Unfortunately, this is not an exhaustive list of these disparaging opinions, nor are these attitudes limited to the first few centuries of the Common Era. Women are not "the devil's gateway," "the root of all evil," "a necessary evil" or "a temple built upon a sewer" and there is nothing natural about women being subject to men. We have allowed ourselves and our faith to be hijacked by men who want to control and subjugate us. It is not the model Jesus practiced. Can you imagine Jesus saying anything as cruel and undeserved to or about the women who traveled with him and ministered to him as these "Saints" and fathers of the Church have said about women? I cannot!

We have been told for centuries we are weaker in mind and body, and we have allowed generalizations of ourselves as the weaker sex. But we know women are not any weaker in mind and body than men.

---

[13] Barbara J. MacHaffie, *Her Story: Women in Christian Tradition* (Minneapolis: Fortress Press, 2006), 110.

Women and men are gifted with strengths, abilities and mental acuity. Depending on age, training and education, a woman might be stronger, more skilled or smarter than any number of men. We have been told we are the more sexually aggressive, but we know this is reality turned on its head in this clear example of male projection.

We have been scapegoated as the reason for original sin, a doctrine articulated by St. Augustine, who thought women were good only for bearing children. We are informed that because of original sin, we must be subjugated to our husbands, not teach in church and hold no position of authority. But these churchmen do not get to make the rules for me or other women. As Romans 8:1 states, "There is therefore now no condemnation for those who are in Christ Jesus. For the law of the Spirit of life in Christ Jesus has set you free from the law of sin and of death." (NRSV) The words of some church fathers are not life-affirming words for women. Since the writing of the epistles of the Christian Scriptures and before, we have been told how to dress, how to wear our hair, what jewelry we can wear and how we should feel about ourselves. I am tired of it. I intend to continue to practice my Christian faith and my belief in a loving, egalitarian God in whose image and likeness I am created.

Biblical Family Values

What are biblical family values? Which biblical family exemplified biblical family values? Which biblical family do we value? The women in Jesus' genealogy all had families which do not mirror what many think of today as biblical family values. Does Sarah's family, in which an old barren woman and a young slave girl give birth to the children of the same man, exemplify biblical values? Is it Jesus' family which typifies biblical family values? His mother was engaged to a man when she became pregnant with Jesus. That man was not the father of her child. The gospels of Matthew and Luke report that Mary was a virgin and that the Holy Spirit was the cause of the pregnancy. Mark and John do not mention this astonishing event, nor does Paul or any other Christian biblical author. Even if we accept that the pregnancy was a miraculous pregnancy, pregnancy before marriage is not a biblical family value that proponents of such values espouse. If we accept the commonly professed conviction that Joseph was an older man and Mary was a young teen, does this reflect biblical family values?

In an attempt to understand what Jesus had to say about family values, I consulted three publications: *Cruden's Complete Concordance*, *The Practical Bible Dictionary and Concordance* and *The Illustrated Dictionary and Concordance of the Bible*. *The Illustrated Dictionary and Concordance of the Bible*, a 1070-page volume, does not list the word family. The other two volumes list only one Christian Scriptural reference to the word family. The author of Ephesians 3:15 speaks of the father from whom every family in heaven and on earth takes their name. Jesus, himself, when he talks about his mother, brothers and sisters, says that those who do the will of God are his family, not necessarily his biological family. Mark 3:33 says, "Whoever does the will of God is my brother and sister and mother." (NRSV) In his critical assessment of the religious leaders found in Matthew 23:9, Jesus warns those listening not to call anyone on earth "father" as we have one father in heaven. Is this representative of biblical family values?

Some of the families mentioned in the Gospels are the sisters Mary, Martha and their brother Lazarus. They were friends of Jesus who appear to be unmarried and live together in Martha's home. Martha appears to be the head of the household. Peter's mother-in-law, brother Andrew and the father who they left working in the boat while they follow Jesus are mentioned. But the wife Peter left to follow Jesus is not. Does leaving your wife, your father and your family business constitute a biblical family value? Jesus and John the Baptist seem to be homeless, celibate men. Jesus is quoted as saying in Matthew 8:20 "The Son of Man has no place to lay his head" and Matthew describes John as one crying in the wilderness, eating locusts and wild honey. Are these biblical family values?

Do we take our instructions on biblical family values from Deuteronomy 21:15, where a man is warned not to show preference to the son of his favorite wife if that son is not the firstborn? Or Deuteronomy 21:18–21, where parents are instructed to take a stubborn and rebellious son to the elders at the gate to be stoned to death? Or, perhaps, we should look to Exodus 21:7, which gives instructions for the selling of a daughter into slavery? No, of course not! These laws and instructions were given at a specific time in history, the late Bronze Age, to a specific group of people, ancient Israel. These laws are not compatible with twenty-first-century American culture.

A call to biblical family values is usually a call for women to retreat from the public sphere and a call for women's submission and subordination in the home and in the church. The words attributed to Jesus in the gospels have little to say about families. The verses employed to support biblical values are those found in the epistles which require the subordination and submission of women. Jesus does not require the subordination and submission of the women who traveled with and ministered to him and the other male members involved in his work.

THE BIBLE

The Bible for Christians, whether ministers, priests or lay persons, remains a great spiritual resource. Understanding who wrote it, to whom it was written, and why it was written are questions which are just as important as the question, "What does the Bible say to me?" As I stated in the introduction, for me, an unexamined faith is not worth living. Therefore, it is of great importance to understand the Book (actually a library) which we call "The Word of God." This is, by no means, an exhaustive examination of biblical formation but a brief overview of how we got our Bible.

The way biblical writers interpret earlier writings influences the way we interpret the Bible. Tradition informs us that Moses wrote the first five books of the Bible. In fact, *The King James Version* of the Bible titles each of those five books The First Book of Moses, The Second

Book of Moses, The Third Book of Moses, etc. Biblical scholarship has made great strides since the time of the writing of the Christian Scriptures. Redaction criticism, form criticism, literary criticism, the historical-critical method, and hermeneutics of suspicion are just some of the methods scholars use to interpret Scripture. "Two hundred and fifty years of historical-critical scholarship have established that Genesis was written over many centuries using oral and written tradition." (NRSV) The other four books attributed to Moses were not written by a single person nor do they represent a single tradition. "Together they have come to belong to our tradition."[15]

There are numerous references in the Christian Scriptures to Moses and the laws he is credited with writing in Genesis, Exodus, Leviticus, Numbers and Deuteronomy. The writers of the Christian Scriptures based their understanding of the Hebrew Scriptures on traditional interpretations, not on biblical scholarship. The writers of the Christian Scriptures were not writing with an eye toward someday having their writings collected into the library that we call the Bible. They were writing to inform and instruct specific communities about the life and message of the man Jesus. Indeed, Jesus' message was not intended to form a new religion but to reform his own religion. Paul transformed the religion of Jesus into a religion about Jesus.

Paul was never a follower of Jesus during the life of Jesus. In fact, he did not know Jesus in Jesus' life. Paul, when we first meet him in Acts 7:58, was a persecutor of the followers of Jesus. At that time, Paul is called Saul. Paul had no written documents about the life and message of Jesus. What Paul did have were the oral testimony of those who believed in Jesus' message and Paul's own somewhat subjective experience on the road to Damascus. The first gospel, Mark, was written at least five years after Paul's first letter to the Thessalonians. Paul had written as many as seven letters before the Gospel of Mark was written. Paul was developing his theology as he went along, in

---

[14] Nancy Corran, written message to author, July 2011.

relationship and reaction to what was occurring in the churches he founded.

The gospels were not written by the men who were friends of Jesus in his life. The names Luke and Mark are not on the lists of the twelve found in Matthew 10:2–4, Mark 3:16–19 or Luke 6:14–16. In fact, the list of the twelve is slightly different in Luke's gospel. Thaddeus is not on Luke's list. Instead Judas, son of James, replaces Thaddeus.

Early church tradition ascribes the Gospel of Mark to John Mark, a disciple of Peter. However, modern biblical scholars find little proof to maintain this tradition. The gospels of Matthew and Luke were written fifty or more years after the life of Jesus. They both use the Gospel of Mark as one of their sources. The writer of Luke admits in Luke 1:1–3 he was not an eyewitness to Jesus. "Since many have undertaken to set down an orderly account of the events that have been fulfilled among us, just as they were handed on to us by those who from the beginning were eye witnesses and servants of the word, I too decided, after investigating everything carefully from the very first, to write an orderly account for you, most excellent Theophilus." (NRSV) Apparently, the author of Luke does not think the other writers have done a very good job. John, the last of the gospels to be written, is dated sixty to eighty years after the life of Jesus. The names given to each gospel are not necessarily the names of the gospel writers.

Jesus' last name is not Christ. Christ is a Greek translation of the Hebrew word for "Messiah" and thus a title, not a name. "'Jesus' is the English equivalent of the Latin version of the Greek rendering of his original Aramaic name, which was Jeheshua or Jeshua, and was probably pronounced (and may actually be spelled) 'Yeshua.'"[16]

There are three repetitions of the story of Paul's conversion on the road to Damascus. When Paul asks the voice that speaks to him out of the light, "Who are you?" the voice answers; "I am Jesus" in Acts

---

[15] Paul Alan Laughlin with Glenna S. Jackson, *Remedial Christianity: What Every Believer Should Know about the Faith, but Probably Doesn't* (Santa Rosa: Polebridge Press, 2000), 77.

9:5 and Acts 26:15 and "I am Jesus of Nazareth" in Acts 22:8. It is Paul who uses the honorarium "Lord" when asking the question. "Jesus calls himself 'Son of God' only in John, the latest and most Christologically developed of the gospels; and the phrase really is commonplace only in the letters of Paul and other New Testament writings, such as Hebrews, which apply it to him."[17]

Paul did not teach the message of Jesus, nor does he write about the life of the historical Jesus. Instead, Paul taught the death and resurrection of Jesus. In First Corinthians 2:2 Paul writes, "When I came to you, brothers and sisters, I did not come proclaiming the mystery of God to you in lofty words or wisdom. For I decided to know nothing among you except Jesus Christ, and him crucified." (NRSV) At the beginning of Jesus' "ministry," Jesus is quoted as saying in Mark 1:15, "The time is fulfilled, and the kingdom of God has come near; repent, and believe in the good news." (NRSV) For Jesus, the reign of God is here and now. It is in this world. Repentance is a call for restoration of relationship with God in God's renewal of Israel.

What many of us do not realize when we talk about the Bible being the word of God is that we do not have any original manuscripts of any of the books in the Bible. We have only copies of copies and translations. The oldest Hebrew manuscripts to be discovered are made up of Dead Sea scroll fragments dating between 250 and 200 B.C.E. As for the Christian Scriptures, our oldest fragment dates from the early Second Century and is written in Greek. It is from John 18:31–33.

Further, the ancient manuscripts we possess do not say exactly the same thing. One example is the Gospel of Mark which ends with verse 16:8 in some manuscripts. Other manuscripts add verses 9–20 with variations. The books of the Bible were written over thousands of years and in diverse locations from Babylon to Rome.

The Hebrew Bible, what many Christians call the Old Testament, did not burst upon the scene in its present form. "The Old Testament's

---

[16] Laughlin, 95.

formation occurred in at least three distinct stages: the Pentateuch or *torah* came together around 400 B.C.E.; the Prophets, which included some historical books, around 200 B.C.E.; and the Writings, which contain many different kinds of books, including the Psalms, perhaps as late as 100 C.E."[18] Second Timothy, written between 100 and 150 C.E. states that, "All Scripture is inspired by God, and is useful for teaching, for reproof, for correction, and for training in righteousness." (NRSV) The writer of Second Timothy is referring to the Hebrew Scriptures. Christian Scriptures had not been collected into a volume at that time.

Like the Hebrew Bible, the Christian Bible developed over several centuries. The Gospels and Epistles were not written in the order in which they appear in our Bible. First Thessalonians is Paul's earliest letter and was written between 50 and 60 C.E. This letter was followed by Philippians, Galatians, First Corinthians, Second Corinthians, Romans and Philemon. The Gospel of Mark, the first canonical Gospel written, was written between 65 and 80 C.E. The last Epistle to become part of our Bible was Second Peter, written between 100 and 160 C.E. Thus, the books that comprise the Christian Scriptures were written over a period of as much as one hundred and ten years.

In 367 C.E., Athanasius, the bishop of Alexandria, wrote an Easter letter to his congregations. His subject was books suitable for reading in the church. There continues to be disagreement about which works were appropriate for instruction in the Church. Even today, the Bibles of Roman Catholics, Greek Orthodox, Russian Orthodox and Protestants differ as to which books are accepted. The Septuagint is an ancient Greek translation of the Hebrew Bible and contains books which Roman Catholics and Greek Orthodox accept as Scripture. Protestants refer to these books as the Apocrypha, meaning "hidden things," and place them between the Hebrew and Christian Scriptures or after the Christian Scriptures. During the Protestant Reformation,

---

[17] Corrine L. Carvalho, *Encountering Ancient Voices: A Guide to Reading the Old Testament* (Saint Paul: Saint Mary's Press, 2006), 17.

Martin Luther excluded these books from the Bible. These disputed books originated with the Greek-speaking Jews in Egypt and were not part of the Scriptures of the Jews in Palestine.

There were many more Gospels and Epistles written during the formative years of the Christian Scriptures. An excellent example comes from a discovery in Egypt, in 1945, of a library known as the *Nag Hammadi Library*. It contains 50 texts, including the Gospel of Thomas. The Gospel of Thomas is dated between 50 and 140 C.E. The Gospel of Mark is dated between 65 and 80 C.E. The writers of these two gospels may have been contemporaries, writing from different perspectives about the life, work and message of Jesus.

Just as we find diversity in the Christian Church today, there was great diversity in the early church. Various groups believed they understood true worship and the true nature of Jesus. Their beliefs differed from what has come to be Orthodox Christianity. The Gnostics, the Marcionites, the Docetists and the Ebionites, to name a few, each had their own inspirational documents which they read in their gatherings. "Those who would argue for the infallibility or the inerrancy of scripture logically should also claim the same infallibility for the churches in the fourth and fifth centuries, whose decisions and historical circumstances have left us with our present Bible."[19]

The invention of printing furthered the stability of the Christian canon. John Wycliffe is recognized as the producer of the first English Bible in 1382. Since that time many men are credited with the translation and revision of the Bible. It is only in the past thirty years that women have been among the contributors on biblical-revision committees. Archaeological discoveries and our understanding of ancient language and culture influence our understanding of the Bible. Add to that the perspective of women, and we arrive at a much richer understanding.

---

[18] Lee Martin McDonald, *The Formation of the Christian Canon* (Nashville: Abingdon Press 1988), 169.

Bible studies focus on how we can apply lessons from the Bible to our life today. Biblical studies concentrate on the historical setting, intention of the author, geographical location, context and audience of the various books of the Bible. Biblical literacy, like literacy in any other area, enhances how we understand and appreciate the wonderful world we live in. Biblical literacy enables us to understand why we believe what we believe.

What Do We Believe About God?

I had a dream recently in which I was walking beside a woman sitting in a wheelchair. She was holding my hand and pointing out all the beauty around us. She wanted to give me a gift. I wanted the gift, but I did not want her to know I wanted the gift, so I wandered away to look at other things. She was an old woman with short, white, spiky hair and a bright, animated smile. Her chair was pushed by a young, beautiful, serene woman with long, dark hair. Her name was Jess. The old woman's name was Greta. Shortly after I wandered off, Jess found me and gave me a pearl ring. The ring was so large it could be worn as a bracelet. She said, "If you hadn't wandered off, there would have been more." I asked her what I should do now. She answered, "Just say thank you."

Unlike most of my dreams, this one was so vivid it stayed with me even after I awoke. Greta, I felt, represented God and Jess represented Jesus. But why, I wondered, would I dream of God as an old woman in a wheelchair? It was a question I contemplated often. Then one morning, during morning prayer, the answer came to me. Greta is the opposite of the image I had been taught of God. From Michelangelo's painting of creation in the Sistine Chapel to the expression "The man upstairs," I have been taught that God is an all-powerful male. Despite the commandment in Exodus 20:4 insisting on imageless worship, we have made an idol of a male image of God.

What makes God male? God is called "The Rock" in Deuteronomy 32:4, which does not make God a rock. The reference is metaphorical.

If I am referred to as a guy, which I often am, as in "Hey you guys?" that does not make me a guy. In Deuteronomy 32:18 God is again referred to as a rock: "You were unmindful of the Rock that bore you; you forgot the God who gave you birth." (NRSV) Rocks, of course, do not give birth. This metaphor is a symbol for the strength and maternal nature of the divine. God is portrayed as a powerful woman who gives birth to her people.

God is also referred to as a woman giving birth in Isaiah 42:14 and Job 38:29. God is credited with comparing God's self to the actions of a nursing mother in Isaiah 49:15 and a comforting mother in Isaiah 66:13.

Jesus uses the simile of a mother hen to describe himself in Matthew 23:37. He is quoted as saying he would have gathered the children of Jerusalem as a mother hen gathers her brood under her wing. In Proverbs 1:20, Wisdom is personified as a woman. In Matthew 11:19, Jesus is quoted as saying, "the Son of Man came eating and drinking, and they say, 'Look, a glutton and a drunkard, a friend of tax collectors and sinners!' Yet Wisdom is vindicated by her deeds." (NRSV) It is to Lady Wisdom that Jesus compares himself. Jesus equates the reign of God with the housekeeping actions of women in the parable of the baking woman and the woman sweeping for the lost coin.

For many women, a male authority figure or a male father figure is not a comforting or safe image. "One in every six American women will be a victim of sexual assault in her lifetime."[20] Incest, by its very definition, is committed by a close family member. "Two-thirds of all rapes are committed by someone the victim knew."[21]

Female imagery for God may, in some instances, be the best image for some women. God is beyond knowing. God is not limited to maleness or femaleness. Romans 1:22–23 says, "Claiming to be wise,

---

[19] "Statistics," *RAINN*. October 3, 2013. http://www.rainn.org/statistics.

[20] *Ibid.*

they became fools; and they exchanged the glory of the immortal God for images resembling a mortal human being or birds or four-footed animals or reptiles." (NRSV) Insisting on male and fatherly imagery for the Divine is foolish, exchanging the immortal God for an image resembling a mortal man.

A hen is female. Men do not give birth to or nurse children. The references to God as something other than a male, father figure may be overshadowed by male generic language, pronouns and the word "father," but the female imagery of the divinely feminine aspects of God are present in both the Hebrew and Christian Scriptures. God is Spirit. God has no body parts to distinguish God as male or female. Humans, both male and female, are referred to in Genesis 1:26 and in Genesis 5:1 as being made in the image and likeness of God.

On the Most Holy Trinity Sunday, the church bulletin at St Joseph's Parish read, "No religion asserts that it has found words to name fully the ineffable mystery of God, for no matter what name we use, God always transcends our limited ability to understand. God is a mystery to be believed, not known." I could not agree more, and yet any language which embraces the feminine in our creator, which there surely must be, is often perceived as idolatrous.

Finally, what do we believe God's relationship is to creation? There are many ways to conceive God's relationship or lack of relationship with creation: transcendentalism, naturalism, rationalism, etc. The four theological types addressed here are Deism, Theism, Pantheism and Panentheism. These types hinge on the concepts of transcendence and immanence. Transcendence is the theology which conceives of God as "being prior to and exalted above the universe, and having being apart from it."[22] In other words, God existed before the universe and is not part of the universe. Immanence is the theology which focuses on "The indwelling presence of God in the world (including

---

[21] *Webster's New Collegiate Dictionary,* 2nd ed., s.v. "transcendence."

man)"[23] and I would add "woman." Deism, Theism, Pantheism and Panentheism each have a different understanding of the relationship between transcendence and immanence. Deists believe God created the universe and withdrew from any further involvement with the creation. God is transcendent. Theists also believe that God created the universe and continues to intervene in human history. Thus, God is both transcendent and immanent.

Pantheism and Panentheism are a little more complicated. I came across this prayer in the chapel of Chapman College in the early seventies. It was written by John Woolman, a Quaker who lived between 1720 and 1772. "I find in my nature a something instinctive which is yet in me even when I do not know; something with which I am alone even as tho it were myself, which is truly nearer to me than myself. This is something so near, so wonderful, yet impossible to understand, must needs be God—There is a principle which is pure, placed in the human mind, which in different places and ages hath had different names; it is, however, pure and proceeds from God. It is deep and inward, confined to no forms, nor excluded from any wo/man when the heart stands in perfect sincerity." This prayer, I believe expresses the essence of Panentheism, God's immanence, which is indwelling, but also God's transcendence, which is more than creation. Paul appears to express Panentheism when he is quoted as saying, in God we live and move and have our being. Pantheism believes that the creation is God. God has no distinction apart from the creation. Simply stated, Panentheism equals God *in* all, Pantheism equals God *is* all.

Where Do We Go from Here?

On Friday, June 23, 2011, my computer opened to show the headline "Americans Like Baby Boys Best." Stephanie Pappas, senior writer for Live Science, writes, "The preference for boys over girls is driven

[22] *Ibid.*, s.v. "immanence."

by men, 49 percent of whom said they'd want a son. Only 22 percent said they'd prefer a daughter."[24] It seems little has changed over the past several thousand years. In a letter from a first-century husband to his wife, he writes, "I beg and entreat you, take care of the little one, and as soon as we receive our pay, I will send it up to you. If by chance you bear a child, if it is a boy, let it be, if it is a girl, cast it out."[25] The difference is that now most women in the Western world are not ordered to cast out their female children.

After the bombings of September eleventh, Americans asked, "Why do they hate us so?" Women could ask the same question. Why do some husbands hate their wives so much that they do not allow the women to have pain medication during the delivery of their child? Why do some men continue to demand the subordination of women in the home and in the church when there is no evidence that this attitude reflects the actions or attitude of Jesus? Televangelist Pat Robertson is quoted by *The Interfaith Alliance* as saying, "I know this is painful for the ladies to hear, but if you get married you have accepted the headship of a man, your husband. Christ is the head of the household and the husband is the head of the wife and that's the way it is, period." He says he knows it is painful but he cannot possibly know how painful! Would a good and just God truly ordain a condition that is painful for women who choose to get married? People in power do not give up their power easily. It appears that some men like to believe in a hierarchy because they have put themselves on top and say the hierarchy is ordained by God and is the natural order of things. As my friend Hilary Christiansen observed, "It is as if they are equating themselves with God."

It is time to teach our daughters and our sons an understanding of religion and Scriptures which does not use the world view of the male

---

[23] Stephanie Pappas, "Americans Like Baby Boys Best," *livescience*, June 23, 2011. http://www.livescience.com/24757-americans-prefer-boys.html.

[24] Editors, "From Child-Killing to Mysticism: Four Examples of the Pluralistic Challenges that Paul Faced," *Christian History* XIV, no. 47 (1995): 25.

writers of the last four thousand years or more to shape our current understanding of the goodness of God and the message of Jesus. It is time to bring an inclusive perspective to the text in order to illuminate it more fully. There is material in the Bible which men, even with the best of intentions, cannot or will not see. There is material in the Bible that women, by virtue of being women, will understand differently than men.

This work is a call for biblical literacy. It is a call for women to interpret the text for themselves, in the light of theological scholarship, archaeological evidence, historical setting and the intention and audience of the author. I was once told that those who do Midrash believe that the words of Scripture and the spaces between the words are sacred. This work is a call to read between the lines, fill in the blanks, finish the unfinished stories, use our God-given wisdom to make sense of text and answer the question, "Why do we believe what we believe?"

Chronological List of Canonical Christian Scriptures

First Thessalonians written between 50 and 60 C.E.

Philippians written between 50 and 60 C.E.

Galatians written between 50 and 60 C.E.

First Corinthians written between 50 and 60 C.E.

Second Corinthians written between 50 and 60 C.E.

Romans written between 50 and 60 C.E.

Philemon written between 50 and 60 C.E.

Colossians written between 50 and 80 C.E.

Hebrews written between 50 and 95 C.E.

Gospel of Mark written between 65 and 80 C.E.

James written between 70 and 100 C.E.

Second Thessalonians written between 80 and 100 C.E.

Ephesians written between 80 and 100 C.E.

Gospel of Matthew written between 80 and 100 C.E.

First Peter written between 80 and 110 C.E.

Gospel of Luke written between 80 and 130 C.E.

Acts written between 80 and 130 C.E.

Apocalypse of John (Revelation) written between 90 and 95 C.E.

First, Second, and Third John written between 90 and 120 C.E.

Gospel of John written between 90 and 120 C.E.

Jude written between 90 and 120 C.E.

First and Second Timothy and Titus written between 100 and 150 C.E.

Second Peter written between 100 and 160 C.E.

Source: http://www.earlychristianwritings.com

BIBLIOGRAPHY

Beach, Eleanor Ferris, and Frederic Pryor. "How Did Adam and Eve Make a Living?" *Bible Review,* XI, no. 2 (April 1995): 38–42.

Benokraitis, Nijole V., and Joe R. Feagin, *Modern Sexism: Blatant, Subtle, and Covert Discrimination.* Englewood Cliffs: Prentice Hall, 1986.

Bradshaw, Rob. "Papias (Early Second Century)." *Theology on the Web.* February 16, 2011. http://www.earlychurch.org.uk/papias.php.

Bridge Building Images, Inc. *Saint Mary Magdalene.* Commissioned by Grace Cathedral, San Francisco: 1989.

Bruce, F. F., *Commentary on Galatians,* New International Greek Testament commentary. Grand Rapids: Eerdmans, 1982.

Byrne S. J., Brendan. *Paul and the Christian Women.* Collegeville: The Liturgical Press, 1988.

Campbell, Joseph, with Bill Moyers. *The Power of Myth.* New York: Doubleday, 1988.

Carvalho, Corrine L. *Encountering Ancient Voices: A Guide to Reading the Old Testament.* Saint Paul: Saint Mary's Press, 2006.

Cole, Dan. "Into the Heart of Paganism: Why did Paul, the traveling missionary, set down roots in Corinth and Ephesus?" *Christian History* XIV, no. 47 (1995): 22.

Dewey, Joanna. "The Gospel of Mark." In *Searching the Scriptures: A Feminist Commentary,* edited by Elisabeth Schussler Fiorenza, 470–509. New York: Crossroad, 1994.

Diamant, Anita. *The Red Tent.* New York: Picador USA, 1997.

Editors. "From Child-Killing to Mysticism: Four Examples of the Pluralistic Challenges that Paul Faced" *Christian History* XIV, no. 47 (1995): 25.

Fletcher, Elizabeth. "Tamar and Judah: Her Story." *Women in the Bible.* June 29, 2011. http://www.womeninthe bible.net /1,5,Tamar_Judah .htm.

Freidan, Betty. *The Feminine Mystique.* New York: W.W. Norton and Company 1984.

Funk, Robert W., and Roy W. Hoover. *The Five Gospels: The Search for the Authentic Words of Jesus.* New York: Macmillan Publishing Company, 1993.

Geitz, Elizabeth Rankin, *Gender and the Nicene Creed.* Harrisburg: Morehouse Publishing, 1995.

Grenz, Stanley J. and Denise Muir Kjesbo. *Women in the Church: A Biblical Theology of Women in Ministry.* Downers Grove: Inter Varsity Press, 1995.

Herzog, William R. *Parables as Subversive Speech: Jesus as Pedagogue of the Oppressed.* Louisville: Westminster/John Knox Press, 1994.

Jones, David. "A Female Apostle?" *The Council for Biblical Manhood and Womanhood.* September 3, 2012, http://www.cbmw.org/ uncategorized/a-female-apostle/.

Josephus, Flavius. *The Complete Works of Josephus.* Trans. William Whiston. Grand Rapids: Kregel Publications, 1981.

Kirby, Peter. "Polycrates Bishop of Ephesus." *Early Christian Writing.* February 2, 2006. http://www.earlychristianwritings.com/text/ polycrates.html.

Kishlansky, Mark, Patrick Geary, and Patricia O'Brien. *Civilization in the West,* 6th ed., vol. 1. New York: Pearson Education, 2007.

Laughlin, Paul Alan with Glenna S. Jackson. *Remedial Christianity: What Every Believer Should Know about the Faith, but Probably Doesn't.* Santa Rosa: Polebridge Press, 2000.

MacHaffie, Barbara J. *Her Story: Women in Christian Tradition.* Minneapolis: Fortress Press, 2006.

Malian, Bruce J. "New Testament Course Book," *Moses Creighton.* September 25, 2013. http://www.mosescreighton.edu/malin/ntstudy/ntcourse/slide14.html.

McDonald, Lee Martin. *The Formation of the Christian Biblical Canon.* Nashville: Abingdon Press, 1988.

Melly, "Misogyny in the Church-EXPOSED." *Geo Cities.* October 16, 2009. http://www.oocities.org/melly4JC/misogyny.html.

Merlo, Alida V., and Joycelyn M. Pollock, eds., *Women, Law and Social Control,* 2nd ed. New York: Pearson Education, Inc., 2006.

Milgrom, Jo. *Handmade Midrash: Workshops in Visual Theology. A Guide for Teachers, Rabbis, and Lay Leaders.* Philadelphia: The Jewish Publication Society, 1992.

Miller, Jason. "Hasidic Newspaper Photoshops Hillary Clinton from Iconic Photo." *The Jewish Week.* May 8, 2011. http://www.thejewishweek.com/blog/jewish_techs/hasidic_newspaper_photoshop_hillary_clinton-iconic_photo.

Mowczko, Marg, "Misogynist Quotes from the Church Fathers and Theologians," *Newlife.* October 3, 2013. http://newlife.id.au/misogynist-quotes-from-church-fathers/.

Newsom, Carol A., and Sharon H. Ringe, eds., *The Women's Bible Commentary.* Louisville: Westminster/John Knox Press, 1992.

Northrup, Christiane. *Women's Bodies, Women's Wisdom: Creating Physical and Emotional Health and Healing.* New York: Bantam Books, 1998.

O'Neil, Cynthia, Peter Casterton, and Catherine Headlam, eds. *Goddesses, Heroes and Shamans: The Young People's Guide to World Mythology*. New York: Scholastic, 1999.

Pagels, Elaine. *The Gnostic Gospels*. New York: Random House, 1979.

Pappas, Stephanie. "Americans Like Baby boys Best," *livescience*. June 23, 2011. http://www.livescience.com/14757-americans-prefer-boys.html.

Parsons, John J. "The Hebrew Names of God-El." *Hebrew for Christians*. November 3, 2010. http://www.hebrew4christians.com/Names_of_G-d/El /el.html.

Plaskow, Judith. *Standing Again at Sinai: Judaism from a Feminist Perspective*. San Francisco: Harper. 1991.

Robinson B. A. "Supportive Passages from the Hebrew Bible (a.k.a. Old Testament)." *Religious Tolerance*. July 29, 2010. http://www.religioustolerance.org.

Schiff, Judith. "Milestones in the Education of Women at Yale." *Yale University*. April 6, 2011. http://www.yale.edu./oir/open/pdf_public_/W009_Enroll.Wom_Milestones.pdf.

Schussler-Fiorenza, Elizabeth. *In Memory of Her: A Feminist Theological Reconstruction of Christian Origins*. New York: Crossroad, 1983.

Staff of the Executive Committee of the SBC. "Southern Baptist and Women Pastors," *Baptist 2 Baptist*. April 10, 2011. http://www.baptist2baptist.net.

"Statistics," *RAINN*. October 3, 2013. http://www.rainn.org/statistics.

Stuart van Wormer, Katherine, and Clemens Bartollas. *Women and the Criminal Justice System*. New York: Pearson Education, Inc., 2007.

"Names of God 6 (El-Shaddai)." *The Parent Company*. February 25, 2011. http://www.theparentcompany.com/awareness_of_god/nog6.htm

Teubal, Savina J. *Sarah the Priestess: The First Matriarch of Genesis*. Athens: Swallow Press/Ohio University Press, 1989.

Torjensen, Karen Jo. *When Women Were Priests: Women's Leadership in the Early Church & the Scandal of their Subordination in the Rise of Christianity.* San Francisco: Harper, 1995.

Williams, Don. *The Apostle Paul & Women in the Church.* Ventura: Regal Books Division. G/L Publications, 1977.

Winter, Miriam Therese. *Woman Wisdom: A Feminist Lectionary and Psalter—Women of the Hebrew Scriptures, Part One.* New York: Crossroad, 1993.

Winter, Miriam Therese. *Woman Witness: A Feminist Lectionary and Psalter—Women of the Hebrew Scriptures, Part Two.* New York: Crossroad, 1992.

Winter, Miriam Therese. *Woman Word: A Feminist Lectionary and Psalter—Women of the New Testament.* New York: Crossroad, 1994.

Wolf, Naomi. *The Beauty Myth: How Images of Beauty Are Used Against Women.* New York: Anchor Books Doubleday, 1991.

Wright, George Ernest, and Floyd Vivian Filson, eds., *The Westminster Historical Atlas to the Bible.* Philadelphia: The Westminster Press, 1974.

BIOGRAPHY

Dr. Paula Trimble-Familetti

Dr. Trimble-Familetti is a passionate advocate for women's rights, inclusive language and biblical literacy. She spent thirty years of her life as an elementary school teacher, ignoring her call to write the stories of biblical women, to advocate for women and to further biblical literacy. She holds a B.A. in Religion from Chapman University, an M.A. in Religion from Liberty University and a Doctor of Ministry in International Feminist Theology from San Francisco Theological Seminary. She has taught Women and Religion and Women's History classes for Chapman University and is past co-convener of the Women's Caucus of the American Academy of Religion. She is a regular contributor to the Words of Faith column in the Desert Sun News. Dr. Trimble-Familetti lives in Indio and Big Bear, California with her husband of thirty years.

Her website is www.DrTrimble-Familetti.com
Blog: whybelieve1.blogspot.com
E-mail: paula.trimblefamiletti@yahoo.com